The Cultivation of New Zealand Native Grasses

The Cultivation of New Zealand Native Grasses

Lawrie Metcalf

My wife, Lena, and I have long had an interest in native grasses and we are particularly fond of the large species of *Chionochloa* or snow grasses. If we had to name a favourite it would have to be the red tussock (*C. rubra*) with which we became so familiar during our time in Southland. It was this fondness for the red tussock which was the genesis of this book. In it I have tried to include all of those native grasses which are commercially available from one source or another. As I embarked on this task I was surprised at just how many different native grasses are being grown by nurseries throughout the country.

Once again I am grateful to Geoff Davidson of Oratia Native Plants, who assisted with the provision of grasses which were not available from other sources and also provided information on their uses. I am also particularly grateful to Lena for her assistance with this project.

A GODWIT BOOK
published by
Random House New Zealand
18 Poland Road, Glenfield, Auckland, New Zealand
www.randomhouse.co.nz

First published 1998, reprinted 2001

ISBN 1 86962 023 2

Production by Kate Greenaway
Printed in Hong Kong

Cover photograph: *Carex comans* 'Frosted Curls'

Contents

Introduction

After many years of various garden fashions in which ornamental grasses have played very little part they are, at last, beginning to attract the long-overdue attention of gardeners. In this country we have an interesting range of native grasses, some of which are exceptionally fine garden plants, and it is pleasing to see the variety of ways in which our native grasses are now starting to be used in both home gardens and public plantings. In line with this increase in interest, more nurseries and garden centres are producing and stocking a wider range of ornamental native grasses.

The term 'grass' is somewhat confusing because not only is it used to refer to the true grasses, but in a broader sense it is also used to refer to rushes, sedges and some similar plants. Some people also use it to include a whole range of quite unrelated plants, largely on the basis that they have long and narrow, strap-like leaves; whether that definition is accepted depends partly on how much of a purist one is. The plants treated in this book are confined to those plant families which are generally thought of as grasses in the broad sense, i.e. Gramineae, Juncaceae, Cyperaceae, Typhaceae and Restionaceae.

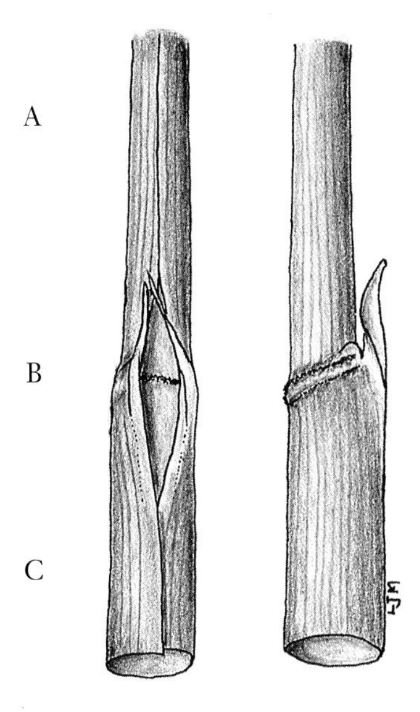

Parts of a grass leaf. (A): leaf blade; (B): ligule; (C): leaf-sheath.

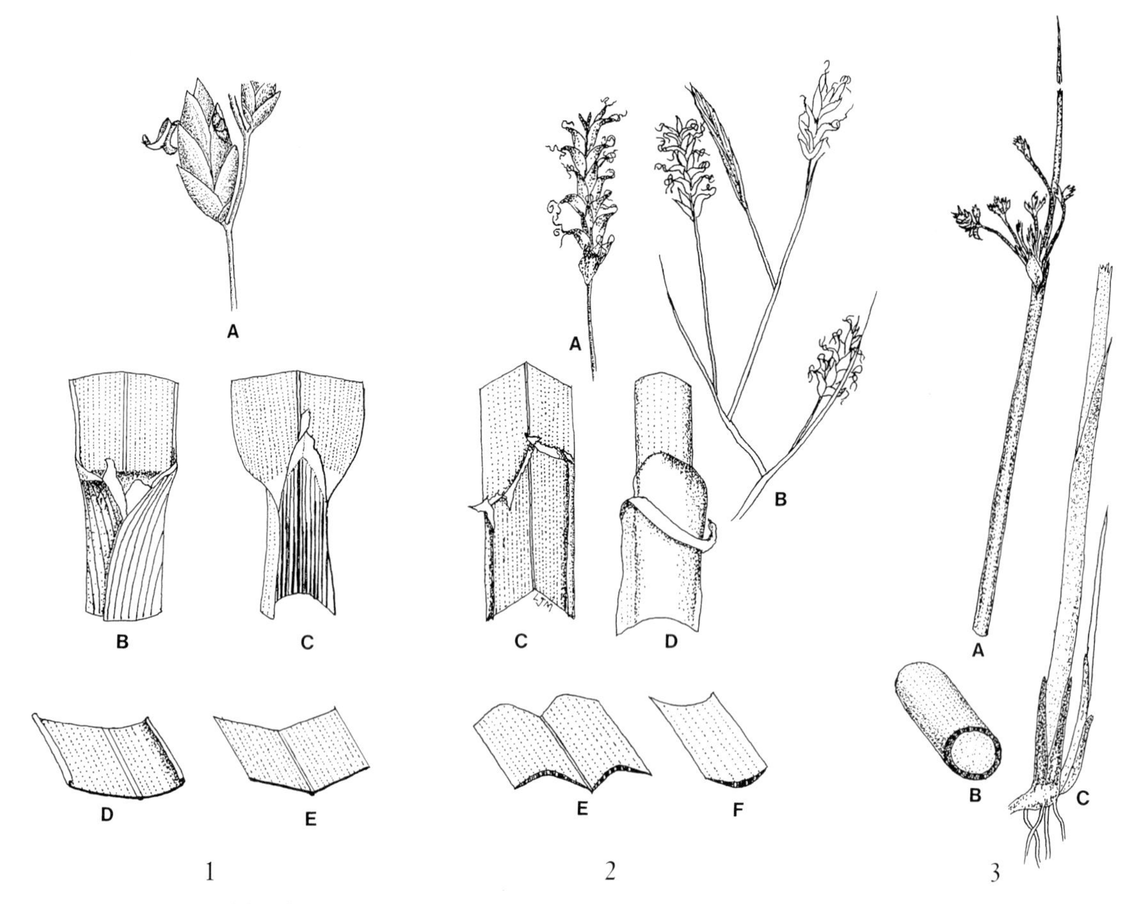

Some of the characters which help to distinguish true grasses, sedges and rushes.
1. True grasses. A: spikelet showing flowers; B: cylindrical sheath and ligule; C: rolled leaf and ligule; D and E: sections of leaf-blades.
2. Sedges. A: flower-spike; B: portion of inflorescence; C: and D: leaf-sheaths; E: section of double-folded leaf; F: section of concave leaf.
3. Rushes. A: portion of stem with inflorescence; B: section of stem; C: base of stem showing diminutive leaves.

Strictly speaking, true grasses are only those plants which belong to the Gramineae family (sometimes referred to as the Poaceae family). Apart from minute differences involving the flowers, true grasses may be distinguished by their stems being round in section, usually hollow, and by the way in which the basal leaf-sheaths split and open down one side so that they can easily be pulled away from the stem. Plants of the rush family (Juncaceae) have round stems which may be hollow or filled, to varying degrees, with a soft pith. Their leaves are mainly basal and may be flat or round in section. Sedges usually have solid stems which are often triangular in section, while their leaf-sheaths are closed so that they completely surround the stems. An old saying which helps to remember one way of distinguishing plants of the sedge family states 'sedges have edges', however that is by no means infallible as the stems of some may be almost rounded. The leaves of sedges are usually grouped around the stem in threes. One or two native rush-like plants belong to the Restio family (Restionaceae), which is an ancient Gondwanaland family now mainly restricted to South Africa, Australia and New Zealand.

The true grasses are one of the most important plant groups on Earth and they are found almost everywhere except for the Polar regions. The domestication of some species for cereal crops, fibre plants and pasture plants was a vital step in the development of modern civilisation. They enabled mankind to progress from loose family groups of hunter-gathers and nomads to the more highly developed social communities living in permanent settlements, in villages and towns.

In New Zealand the native grasslands occur mainly on the central Volcanic Plateau of the North Island and down the eastern side of the South Island. Above the bush-line of the North, South and Stewart Islands grasslands also occur but seldom on the same scale as they do in the more open country at lower altitudes.

Our grasslands fall broadly into two distinct plant formations according to the sizes of their main tussock components. These two formations are respectively known as low-tussock grassland and tall-tussock grassland. Low-tussock grasslands occur mainly on the eastern sides of both islands from sea level to about 1200 m. Tall-tussock grasslands can occur up to 1500 m or more, while in the southern part of the South Island they occur down to sea level.

The sight of whole hillsides or large tracts of rolling country covered with tawny or reddish-coloured tussocks rippling and waving in the wind is one of the great sights of the New Zealand back country and is in distinct contrast to the cultured meadows of Europe.

'I see again the upland wilds,
Stern, rugged, bleak, and bare;
The strong winds sweep o'er the hill sides steep
And the tussocks toss in the icy air
Silver and gold in the changing light,
Gold and silver far up on the heights
Of the mountain wild and bare.'

David McKee Wright

Gardening with native grasses

Purchasing plants

One of the most important points when purchasing grasses for your garden is to choose only those species that are suitable for your particular situation. Most grasses are hardy throughout the country, but some are less tolerant of frost, others will not tolerate salt-laden coastal winds and some will not thrive in extremely dry soils. If in doubt, seek advice.

Do not impulsively buy the first grass you see on display in the garden centre. Check first that it will be suitable and not be too large for your garden. For example, *Carex comans* 'Frosted Curls' is usually sold in PB5 bags or similar and gives no indication of its final size. When planted in the garden it will eventually assume its rather sprawling habit and cover an area up to about 1 m across. Is the foliage the right colour, does it have the right habit of growth and will it fit in with, and complement, the plants which will be its neighbours?

Always choose young and vigorous plants which are well grown and try to avoid old plants which have obviously been in the container (and in stock) too long. Old plants will eventually make good growth, but younger and more vigorous plants usually make quicker growth.

Finally, there is one habit which many garden-centre owners have which I find mildly annoying. The drawn-out tips of the leaves of nearly all grasses usually die. This is a natural feature of any grass and, in my opinion, does not detract from the appearance of the plant. Many garden-centre owners seem to feel that the dead leaf tips spoil the plant's appearance and cut them off, leaving them looking shorn.

Soils

In general most grasses are not fussy as to soil and, in fact, some actually perform much better when grown in a poor soil; plant them in a rich soil and they grow out of character. Quite a number will perform very well in soils of indifferent quality, although they may grow much better in a good or improved soil.

Apart from those species, such as the silver tussock (*Poa cita*) and fescue tussock (*Festuca novae-zelandiae*), which are better in low-fertility soils (otherwise they grow out of character), most grasses will appreciate a better-quality soil which has had some organic material added. This applies more particularly to newly planted grasses; once well established most can then be left to become accustomed to a leaner soil. When adding organic material to the soil, be careful not to overdo it—too much nitrogen may cause the foliage to become lank and floppy.

The majority of grasses prefer a well-drained soil, and even some of those which naturally grow in wet soils will often grow perfectly well in drier, well-drained soils. Heavy soils which become wet during the winter or periods of wet weather may need to have their drainage improved before planting.

Planting

With all nursery-grown grasses being sold in containers, it is possible to plant them at most times of the year. It is only in those areas that experience dry summers that planting should be delayed until moister conditions prevail, although even then grasses can be planted if they are watered until they become established.

As a general rule, however, the best time for planting is from autumn until mid-spring. Grasses planted during that period quickly become established and make good growth. The exception to this is in districts which experience severe winter conditions, especially when prolonged freezing occurs. In those districts planting is best delayed until spring so that the plants have all spring and summer to become established. Very hardy species could be planted during early autumn; however, where there are doubts as to the hardiness of a particular species, it should not be planted until spring.

Before planting it is essential to make sure that the soil has been cleared of any weeds, particularly weed grasses which could become a pest in an ornamental planting. In particular, weeds with underground rhizomes, such as sheep's sorrel (*Rumex acetosella*), and perennial grasses, such as twitch or couch (*Agropyron repens*) and browntop (*Agrostis tenuis*), are the worst. Even tufted grasses such as rye grass (*Lolium perenne*) and Yorkshire fog (*Holcus lanatus*) can be a problem if they take root in a clump of ornamental grass.

At this stage it is worth taking a little extra time to ensure that these weeds have been eradicated before planting. Working over the soil with a garden fork can be very effective for this. After the first weeding wait for two or three weeks for any pieces of root to sprout and then carefully fork them out. If the soil was dry at the time of the first weeding, give it a thorough watering to encourage any remaining pieces of root to break into new growth. If the weed infestation is severe, it may be necessary to use a suitable non-residual herbicide, such as glyphosate.

Planting grasses is quite easy and it is only necessary to keep one or two simple guidelines in mind. Practically all grass plants are sold in containers of some kind, and it is only when transplanting those already growing in your own garden that you will be dealing with open-ground plants.

- Always thoroughly soak the root-ball in a bucket of water.
- Remove the plant from its container and, with a sharp stick or something similar, roughen the outside of the root-ball to loosen some of the roots; this encourages them to root more quickly into the surrounding soil.

- Do not plant so deep that the crown of the plant is buried well below the surface of the ground. Many plants, and that includes grasses, will not tolerate being planted too deeply.
- At the same time do not make the planting hole so shallow that the top of the root-ball is above ground level or showing on the surface. This will allow the root-ball to quickly dry out and will harm the plant. Ideally, the top of the root-ball should be just below the surface of the ground.
- If the soil is at all dry, water the newly planted grasses immediately, as the fine root systems of many species can be particularly prone to drying out.
- Mulching around newly planted grasses, in addition to reducing maintenance, can help them get off to a good start.

Spacing

Many grasses create the best effect when planted in groups of one species. Others, particularly some of the bolder ones, can be effective when planted as individual specimens. Spacing is really a matter of personal preference and what effect is desired; if a quick effect is required, then plants should be placed more closely than normal. As a general rule-of-thumb it can be assumed that the ultimate width of most grass plants will be approximately equal to their height. Therefore plants of a species which grows to about 60 cm tall should be spaced about 60 cm apart. The limitations of one's budget also come into the equation and it may be necessary to plant at wider spacings and wait a little longer for them to make the necessary growth.

Mulching

As with most other plants, mulching around grasses helps to give them a good start and make subsequent maintenance much easier. It can also provide a more pleasant appearance than just bare earth.

In addition to helping to retain moisture in the soil during dry periods, a good mulch also helps to reduce the surface temperature of the soil during the heat of summer. It will not completely eliminate the necessity for weeding but it will reduce weed growth to a minimum. During winter in colder districts a mulch can be beneficial in helping to protect the soil against excessive freezing.

Suitable mulching materials are bark, a mixture of wood chips and bark, straw (particularly pea straw), leaves and gravel. Materials such as straw and leaves gradually decay to help improve the surface layer of soil.

Maintenance

One of the great advantages of growing ornamental grasses is the fact that they generally require very little in the way of care and attention. If the species have been properly selected for the situation, they can be almost maintenance free.

Newly planted grasses may need to be regularly watered for a short period until they have become established, but apart from that, most should not need watering. If the soil is naturally very dry, or during prolonged dry spells in summer, some species may need to be watered.

Some overseas authors advocate annually cutting back grasses close to ground level, usually in spring just before new growth appears. That may be all very well with some exotic grasses but it certainly does not suit many of our native grasses. In any case very few of them need it. *Anemanthele* or wind grass can be very slow to recover if cut back to near ground level.

What is very important is to groom the plants once a year, in order to remove much of the old foliage. Grooming is probably best carried out during the late winter or early spring. With some species it is possible to remove old foliage simply by combing through the tufts with your fingers, but with others it may be more effective to use a small rake. It is quite easy to make a suitable rake; all that is required is a piece of wood 50 x 25 mm, about 10–12 cm long, to which a short handle has been fixed. For the tines hammer in about ten 40 or 50 mm nails.

After a few years the tufts of some grasses can become thickly matted as the tuft increases in size, and the stems in the centre of the plant have to grow longer to allow their leaves to grow out to the light. This can apply particularly to some of the smaller tussocks such as *Festuca coxii*, *Poa colensoi* and similar species. It can also apply to some of the sedges. While an annual grooming can help to keep plants in good condition, ultimately they may reach the stage where they need to be rejuvenated. When that happens the plant or plants should be dug out of the ground and divided.

Propagation

In general, most native grasses are easily propagated, either from seed or by division. Providing seed is available, it is possible to propagate large numbers of the species without having to disturb the parent plant. In fact, for some grasses it is the most practical way. When it comes to propagating named cultivars or selected clones of ornamental grasses, many do not come true from seed, and the only way to ensure uniformity is to propagate by division.

Seed

For the reward of growing your own grasses from seed, and the excitement of watching their progress from seed sowing until the plants are large enough to set out in the garden, propagating grasses from seed is a very worthwhile thing to do.

Fresh seeds of some grasses will germinate within about 10–20 days, while others may take quite a bit longer. The seeds of some species are light sensitive and, consequently, the containers of sown seed should be kept in fairly well-lit conditions for germination, shaded only from direct sunlight. Seed can be sown as soon as it has been harvested, but sometimes better results are obtained if it is held in dry storage for 4–8 weeks before sowing. Older seed may take longer to germinate than freshly harvested seed.

Anemanthele and most species of *Chionochloa*, as well as a number of other grasses, have very fine seeds. They should be scattered over the surface of the seed-sowing medium and either not be covered or be covered with just the merest suggestion of some of the medium. Larger seeds should have a covering of seed-sowing medium sieved over them.

Once the seedlings are large enough to handle they should be pricked out into containers for growing on; generally, that is when they have made 2–3 or 3–4 true leaves. If the seed has been sown fairly thickly and there has been good germination, it is often better to prick out small clumps of seedlings rather than individuals. When they have made sufficient growth they can be put into pots for growing on. At that stage, or when they are even larger, the clumps can be divided.

Depending on the species and seed source, some grasses can be quite variable when grown from seed, and if it is desired to propagate a number of plants which are reasonably like their parent, then division may be preferable. On the other hand, by raising grasses from seed it is often possible to select variations which are more desirable from a horticultural point of view.

Division

This is the easiest means of propagation as it is simply a matter of lifting the grass from the ground and then separating its crown into a number of pieces. With the smaller tussocks it may be possible to pull them apart with one's hands, or a knife may be required to help separate the pieces. With larger plants two garden forks will be necessary. Push the two forks into the tussock, back to back, and then pull their handles apart so that the tussock is gradually divided into two clumps. That causes the least damage to the plant and its root system. Repeat this process until the required number of divisions have been obtained.

For re-planting, use only the more vigorous pieces from the outside of the plant and discard the remainder, unless a greater number of new plants is required. Divisions for re-planting need not be too large; pieces that can conveniently be held in a partly closed hand should be large enough for most purposes. Unless the divisions are to be grown on in containers, do not make them too small otherwise they will take too long to recover and make good plants again.

Grasses may be divided at various times of the year, but the optimum times are during autumn (late March–late April) and spring (late August–about mid-October). If done early enough in the autumn, newly planted divisions will be able to produce new roots and become established before winter sets in. Spring division should not be left too late and is best carried out just as the new growth appears. On plants with long and floppy foliage it is better to cut it back by one-third or a half to help the new plant to recover. It also makes it tidier until some good new foliage has grown. Smaller grasses with shorter leaves may not need to have their foliage cut back at all. When dividing plants outside of the recommended times it is preferable to cut back the foliage on all divisions.

Grasses which show signs of coming into flower should not be divided because root activity is at its lowest at that time. Wait until flowering has finished before attempting division.

If dry conditions are likely to prevail, newly planted divisions will benefit from regular watering until they become established and new leaves appear.

Landscaping with native grasses

Apart from the fact that they are native, there are a number of valid reasons for utilising grasses in landscape design. They are relatively easy to maintain and most are fairly self-sufficient plants, and there are species and varieties which are suitable for almost any situation in the garden.

Grasses are also attractive throughout the four seasons of the year, although in early spring some may show the effects from winter; however, as summer approaches they soon assume a good appearance again. Some are exceptionally beautiful when they flower and their plumes can remain attractive long after flowering has finished. They also exhibit variation in colour and form throughout the year, and can be very effective during the winter months in helping to enliven the landscape.

By their very nature, grasses also bring a natural element into the garden. They introduce a sense of freedom and movement which many other plants do not possess, and when associated with perennials and shrubs they help to create a scene which suggests untrammelled nature. They will move with just a breath of wind, and to see large clumps of grasses swaying and rippling in the breeze can be very evocative of the open country.

While grasses do not provide colour in the way that annual or perennial flowers do, their range of foliage colours is of great value in the garden, particularly by way of contrast.

Few have strong colours, although the species of *Uncinia* are a lovely reddish or reddish brown colour, *Elymus solandri* has striking blue-grey foliage and that of *Festuca coxii* is bluish. In the main the colours are subtle and muted, but that is not to say they are dull, for they include an amazing spectrum of hues. The various sedges are particularly effective, while plants such as the red tussock (*Chionochloa rubra*) can exhibit a wonderful range of shades under different light conditions.

The attractive textures and simple, strongly linear forms of grasses enable them to be combined with a wide range of garden plants to create some very interesting and pleasing effects. Using the rather stiff, vertical lines of *Festuca novae-zelandiae* with the more flowing effect of, say, *F. coxii* or *Carex comans* 'Frosted Curls' could be striking.

Grasses can also be used to provide focal points in ground-cover plantings as well

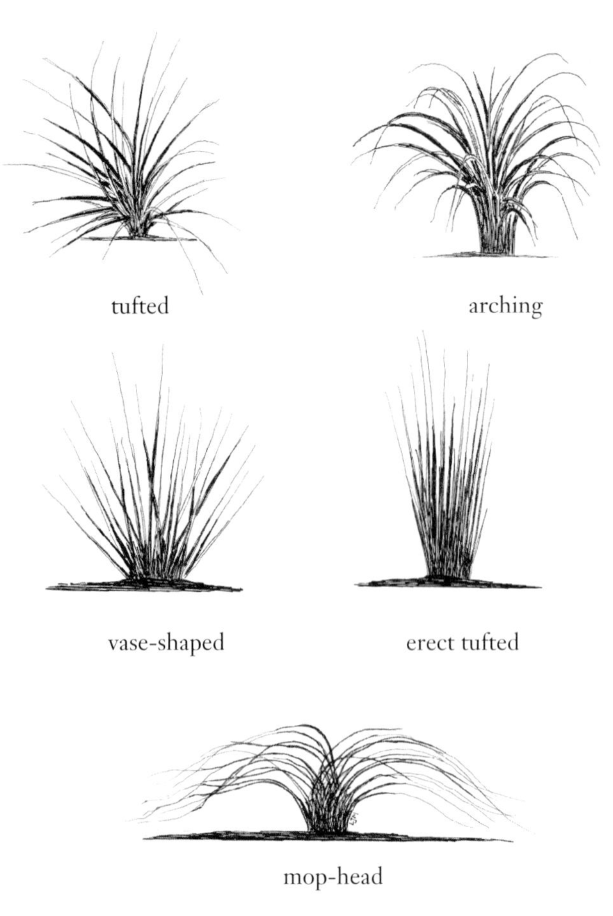

The growth forms of grasses.

as creating colour contrasts. For example, one or two plants of *Festuca* "Banks Peninsula" set in a ground-cover of the purple-leaved biddi biddi (*Acaena inermis* 'Purpurea') could provide an interesting colour combination as well as a contrast of foliage and form. There are numerous combinations which can be tried and they are limited only by one's imagination.

Specimen planting

The larger species of native grasses, in particular, can be most effective when used as accent plants or for featuring as individual specimens. Some, such as the toetoe (*Cortaderia*), hunangamoho (*Chionochloa conspicua*) and snow grasses (*Chionochloa* species), are bold enough to stand as single specimens, thus providing a focal point in particular parts of the garden. Where space permits, consideration should be given to planting groups of a particular species for a really bold effect.

Large grasses associate well with shrubs and with large plantings of perennial plants. *Cortaderia*, *Chionochloa conspicua* and *C. rubra*, as well as some other larger species, can also be used to provide a screen or background in some parts of the garden.

Where space is somewhat limited even some of the medium-sized species, such as *Anemanthele lessoniana*, *Carex buchananii* and *Poa cita*, can be used effectively for specimen planting. *A. lessoniana*, in particular, can be striking when planted in mass.

Ground-cover

When thinking of grasses as ground-cover plants many people tend to consider only the smallest species suitable. However, in the correct situation the larger species can also be quite appropriate. When grasses only are used as a ground-cover they can provide interesting, delicate effects, playing a harmonising role rather than being the dominant feature.

Suitable species for growing under the shade of trees are *Anemanthele*, some members of the genus *Carex*, *Microlaena avenacea* and *Poa anceps*. In open situations the choice is greater, and the genera *Festuca*, *Carex*, *Elymus* and *Poa* will provide some very useful plants. In some situations larger species such as *Chionochloa flavicans* are most effective as a ground-cover.

Imagine the effect of the lovely blue-grey *Festuca coxii* when closely planted to form a ground-cover in an open situation such as around a patio, near a pool or in the front of a border. Some of the carexes are striking when planted in mass as a ground-cover. *Carex testacea*, *C. comans* 'Frosted Curls', *C.* 'Greenie' and selected forms of *C. flagellifera* are all worth considering.

In some situations grasses can be used in combination with carpeting plants to provide a most effective ground-cover—for example, a few spaced plants of *Festuca matthewsii* or a good form of *Poa colensoi* with a carpet of *Acaena inermis* 'Purpurea' growing between.

Rock gardens

Some of the smaller native grasses are ideal for growing in rock gardens. They can be used as specimen plants in their own right to provide interest during those times of the year when many rock-garden plants have passed their best. Alternatively, they can be used to provide a more pleasing and ecologically functional association in which they give shade and shelter to other plants. They can also help to protect the root zones of other plants from excessive heat and drying, very much as they do in their natural habitat.

Watersides and damp places

There is something about the association of grasses and water which captures the imagination. Perhaps it is the memory of some favourite place where grass overhangs the edge of a pond or slow-flowing stream. No matter what, grasses and water arouse visions of peacefulness and tranquillity.

Planting grasses in a waterside situation softens the division between land and water and integrates the two. In general, grasses which have a flowing habit provide a more natural effect, and the picture is further enhanced when a breeze causes movement. Some of the sedges, such as *Carex secta* and *C. virgata*, are particularly suited for waterside planting, while *Chionochloa conspicua*, *C. flavicans* and *C. rubra* are also ideal species for such situations.

Grasses which have a stiffer habit can be planted close to the water's edge because of the interesting reflections they cast in the water. *Sporodanthus traversii*, *Leptocarpus similis* and rushes such as *Juncus gregiflorus* are species which will provide that vertical accent.

Quite a number of grasses are tolerant of or prefer to grow in damp places, and they can be useful when it is difficult finding other plants which will succeed in the situation. Probably foremost among them are the sedges. *Carex secta* and *C. virgata* have already been mentioned, but others such as *C. trifida*, *C. chathamica*, *C. dissita* and *C. flagelllifera* are all suitable. The large tussocks, *Chionochloa conspicua* and *C. rubra*, can also be grown in damp places. If a larger grass is desired, or where space permits, any *Cortaderia* species could be used.

Shady places

Although many people think of grasses as plants of open country, there are those which naturally grow in forest or other shady places, while others are tolerant of lightly shaded conditions.

For growing under the shade of trees we can do no better than to look at one or two of our forest grasses. The bush rice grass (*Microlaena avenacea*) and *Poa anceps* can be used to fill places where it is difficult to establish other plants. Another excellent species is *Anemanthele lessoniana*, which will make a dense and attractive ground-cover.

Coastal gardens

When considering grasses for coastal gardens one's thoughts almost invariably turn to gardens that are exposed to the full force of the elements and have little or no shelter. Burning salt-laden winds, droughts, sandy soils (if close to a sandy beach) or sun-baked clay soils (if on hilly areas) are the main problems which can occur.

Some gardens in coastal areas may be like this, but in many instances they do have some degree of shelter, while others may be quite sheltered. Generally, the further back from the actual shore-line, the more shelter a garden is likely to have. However, in spite of that, occasional severe storms can create havoc, even in a relatively protected coastal garden.

The number of native grasses which are really suitable for coastal gardens is rather limited, although with good shelter more can be included. Perhaps the most obvious choice is the pingao (*Desmoschoenus spiralis*), which grows naturally on sand dunes, but that is not a requirement for growing it in a garden. The silvery sand grass (*Spinifex sericeus*) is another which is useful for coastal gardens, where it should be grown in an open situation. Surprisingly, *Chionochloa rubra* is quite happy in windy, coastal conditions providing it has a reasonably moist soil. Other suitable grasses are *Austrofestuca*, *Carex comans*, *C. testacea*, *C. trifida* (requires moist conditions), *Chionochloa bromoides*, *Cortaderia*, *Elymus* and *Leptocarpus*.

Natural or wild gardens

Those people who have a passion for planting their gardens entirely with native plants may like to consider planting one area solely with native grasses, or predominantly native grasses interspersed with a few shrubs and other plants. This form of gardening is becoming more popular and, when well done, can be most effective.

As well as a feeling of naturalness, such plantings are attractive and interesting the year round. However, it is from midsummer through to the winter when they really come into their own. This is when grasses such as the beautiful blue *Festuca coxii*, red tussock (*Chionochloa rubra*) and *Carex testacea* become a feature, hinting of open grassy places in the country.

Such plantings naturally grow best in reasonably good soils, but such is the tolerance of most grasses that they will succeed quite well in poorer soils. If the soil can be improved with the addition of some humic material, so much the better. Even a good mulching with pea straw, partly rotted straw (not hay, which has too many unwanted grass seeds in it) or compost will do a great deal to help.

Environmental plantings

These days more attention is being paid to re-creating areas of former native vegetation or enhancing existing, but perhaps degraded, areas of natives, and people are also beginning to recognise the importance of grasslands and wetlands when it comes to environmental plantings. It is becoming common practice to plant only those species which are or were originally native to the area, as well as ensuring that the plants have been propagated from locally sourced material. Fortunately, there are some nurseries which can supply such plants, but they are still few and far between.

The first thing to bear in mind when considering an environmental planting is to not plant more than can be easily looked after until the plants are sufficiently well established to look after themselves. Usually that means a period of two to three years or maybe a little longer, depending on how well they grow.

If troublesome weeds are present in the area, it may be necessary to spot spray the planting positions with a herbicide such as glyphosate. For those people who do not like using chemicals of any kind, the only alternative is time-consuming hand weeding, which can be quite daunting for extensive plantings.

Distances between plants depends on the species, but generally they should be sufficiently close that they will soon merge to make a dense cover. One of the worst mistakes is to plant too far apart. Not only does it allow smothering weeds to become established but the final effect will be far from desirable.

The other kind of planting which is included under this heading is that which assists with the treatment of waste water such as the grey water from a house or the effluent from a septic tank. Some suitable species for this kind of planting are *Baumea articulata*, *Schoenoplectus validus* and *Typha orientalis*.

Containers

Some grasses are ideal for growing in containers. This is a particularly useful way of growing them if space is limited or if it is desired to have them in close association with the house, such as on a patio or near a pool. Their shape and form mean that they fit in well with their surrounds as well as in a variety of containers.

Grasses with blue or blue-green foliage are attractive in terracotta pots, whereas orange or reddish-coloured grasses are probably better in a container of some other colour. The red tussock (*Chionochloa rubra*) is particularly effective in a container.

It is important to have a good potting mix. Some proprietary mixes are satisfactory but those which are purely peat based are less suitable. As long as peat is kept moist there is no problem, but it can very quickly dry out and once dry, is extremely difficult to re-wet because it repels water. Even the use of water-retaining agents may not completely solve the problem.

My own preference is to use bark-based potting mixes which do not have the same propensity for quickly drying out and also have a bit of substance to them. Providing they have sufficient slow-release fertiliser in them, plants will remain in good condition for quite some time before they require supplementary feeding. However, all plants grown in containers will eventually require regular feeding.

In time, when plants begin to show obvious signs of deterioration, they should be re-potted. At the same time it may also be advisable to divide them and re-pot a vigorous young division.

Associating other plants with native grasses

While a garden devoted entirely to grasses can be attractive and interesting, only a few gardeners are likely to go to that extent, and most will prefer to mix plants so that they have a variety of foliage types, forms and colours. Using grasses in association with other plants gives great opportunities for providing contrasting and complementary effects, particularly if completely different leaf shapes and plant forms are included. At the same time the use of flowering plants should not be overlooked.

Possibly the most common mistake that many people make is to assume that grasses should automatically be associated with plants which have grassy or sword-like foliage. In fact, nothing could be further from the truth—the resulting effect will be too much of the same thing. This is not to say that such plants should never be planted together but just that it should be done with discretion. Plants such as the renga renga (*Arthropodium cirratum*) and flaxes (*Phormium tenax* and *P. cookianum*) and their various cultivars can and do go very well with grasses, but the effect is often heightened and improved if some broad-leaved plants are also included.

It may sound like heresy, but native grasses do not have to be associated with only native plants. They complement, and are complemented by, a wide range of exotic garden plants and should be associated with whatever plants suit the situation. Plants with bold or rounded foliage, such as *Hosta*, *Brachyglottis* 'Leith Gold', *Pseudopanax laetus* and *Trachystemon*, really help to emphasise the slender and graceful lines of most grasses.

Important attributes to note when using other plants with grasses are colour, form and texture.

Colour is one of the most important aspects because it makes an immediate and powerful impression. However, it is a very personal thing; some people love bright and strong colours while others prefer softer shades. Colour should be used to enhance the planting scheme and not as an end in itself.

It is possible to create contrasting effects by placing two different colours together. Alternatively, more subtle tonal effects can be obtained by using different shades of the same colour. For example, a lime-green or yellow-green combined with a darker green provides a more subtle contrast. Pay attention to creating the right colour effects and any other faults may be less obvious.

The forms of broad-leaved plants and grasses which are to be grown together must also be considered. If the grass has an erect form it can be planted with prostrate or carpeting plants, or it could be planted with something which has a more flowing habit.

The textures of broad-leaved plants and grasses to be used together also needs be borne in mind. Will the texture of one contrast with the other to provide a pleasing effect?

Trees and shrubs

Often there is a distinct contrast between grasses and trees and shrubs, particularly evergreens. The deeper greens of some evergreens can be used effectively to contrast with a lighter-foliaged grass. Some of the larger grasses can be combined with shrubs to form a screen, creating a break between two parts of the garden. *Cortaderia* species and *Chionochloa conspicua* can be used with trees and shrubs such as *Pittosporum*, *Olearia*, *Chamaecyparis*, *Escallonia* and some of the larger hebes as a screen. Grasses also help to fill the gaps between trees and shrubs as well as adding to the variety of forms and textures.

Lower-growing grasses can be used as a ground-cover beneath trees and the larger shrubs. Forest-inhabiting species, such as *Anemanthele lessoniana*, *Carex dissita*, *C. solandri*, *Microlaena avenacea* and *M. stipoides*, are suitable for such purposes.

One group of shrubs which is ideal for associating with grasses are the hebes—there is a hebe for almost any situation. Not only do they vary from large shrubs to prostrate ones only a few centimetres high, but there are also some very fine flowering species and cultivars which produce a display over most of the year. Their foliage is similarly variable in colour and form, ranging from small box-like leaves to much larger leaves, from greens to greys, grey-greens and purplish or variegated foliage. The whipcord hebes, with their conifer-like appearance, provide a completely different dimension; their colour varies from shades of green to greenish yellows and a rich gold or ochre colour. With such a range to choose from there are almost limitless possibilities for combining hebes with grasses.

Among native grasses some colours are not well represented—for example, silver, purples, yellow and cream—and the use of coloured-foliaged trees and shrubs provides the opportunity to bring missing colours into the planting scheme. Both purple and yellow are dominant colours and need to be used carefully in the landscape, but they can also create effective and dramatic contrasts. Silver and cream are less dominant and provide much softer effects; creams, in particular, can bring a freshness into the planting scheme.

Examples of suitable trees and shrubs in these colours are:

Artemisia arborescens
Brachyglottis Dunedin Hybrids
'Leith Gold'
Cotinus coggyria 'Grace'
Dodonaea viscosa 'Purpurea'
Corokia x *virgata* 'Sunsplash'
Griselinia littoralis 'Variegata'

Hoheria populnea 'Alba Variegata'
Lophomyrtus x *ralphii* 'Kaikoura Dawn'
'Variegata'
Pittosporum tenuifolium variegated cultivars such as 'Irene Paterson' and 'Stirling Gold'
Podocarpus nivalis
Robinia pseudoacacia 'Frisia'
Santolina chamaecyparissus

Trees and shrubs with ornamental berries or fruits should not be forgotten. Their fruits are usually produced during the autumn or winter when other interest can be lacking. *Corokia* is particularly good in this respect because the cultivars of *C.* x *virgata* normally hold their fruits right through until almost the end of the winter. Many other trees and shrubs, both native and exotic, have good displays of fruits, most in warm colours which would complement many grasses, particularly those in the warmer tones.

Herbaceous plants

Herbaceous plants, particularly those that flower, give tremendous scope for creating interesting effects and contrasts. However, remember that most plants flower for only a limited period and that foliage features will be necessary for the rest of the year.

There are some very fine plants with bold or interesting foliage and some of the most noteworthy are the hostas. Unfortunately they are winter dormant, but suitable grasses accompanying them will help to fill the gap left by the hostas. While some native plants are excellent foliage plants, the choice is really a bit limited and some of the interesting species are not suitable for general garden cultivation.

Arthropodium cirratum (renga renga) is a most versatile plant. Forms from the offshore islands have particularly bold and handsome foliage; they also have a very good floral display. *Celmisia mackaui* is another useful plant with attractive foliage and the distinction of being one of the most reliable celmisias in the garden. Other of the larger *Celmisia* species can also be used where they can be successfully grown.

Astelia provides the gardener with some excellent companion plants for grasses. The larger species have a boldness which contrasts very well with some grasses, and they are sufficiently different to not appear grass-like. The forest-dwelling *A. fragrans* can be used under trees to associate with *Microlaena avenacea* and *Poa anceps*. The very bold and silvery *A. chathamica* will grow in more open situations, and some of the medium-sized grasses could be planted around it. Alternatively, why not plant larger species such as *Chionochloa conspicua*, *C. rubra* or *C. flavicans* so that they complement each other? *A. nervosa* is a variable and versatile species which should not be overlooked. In its natural habitat it frequently forms effective associations with some of the *Chionochloa* species.

Ferns are another group of plants that people tend to overlook in planting schemes. Where grasses are being grown under trees, what more charming accompaniment is there than ferns? Quite a good range is available from specialist nurseries, and some of our native ferns are ideal for grouping with grasses. Suitable and reliable species are *Asplenium bulbiferum* (hen and chicken fern), *A. oblongifolium*, *Blechnum discolor* (crown fern), *Polystichum richardii* and *P. vestitum* (prickly shield fern). Grasses to associate with them include *Anemanthele lessoniana*, *Microlaena avenacea*, *M. stipoides* and *Poa anceps*.

Ground-cover plants

While virtually any plant can be a ground-cover, in this context the term is being used in a narrower sense to denote lower-growing plants which are generally no more than 10 cm high, although under some circumstances they can be higher.

Ground-covers provide the gardener with endless opportunities for planting schemes in which grasses form the focal point. For example, *Acaena inermis* creates an attractive mat or carpet. If plants of a flowing grass such as *Festuca coxii* are interspersed through the mat of *A. inermis*, there is a mix of contrasting foliage, form and colour, while the acaena provides an attractive background for the fine leaves of *Festuca coxii*. As an alternative, the taller, erect and narrow *Festuca novae-zelandiae* could be used to provide a completely different effect.

One ground-cover which goes particularly well with some grasses is the native alpine hard fern (*Blechnum pennamarina*). It is a charming little fern, particularly when it is putting forth its young, reddish-coloured fronds in the spring.

There are many other suitable ground-cover plants but particular mention should be made of *Pimelea urvilleana*, which forms dense mats of sage-green foliage and has clusters of small white flowers in late spring. It is excellent for an under-planting with grasses. The various species of *Leptinella* are also good ground-cover plants, and they have a range of foliage colours and forms which allows for some interesting effects. The species most commonly available are *L. calcarea* and its green form, *L. rotundata*, *L. traillii* and *L. squalida* 'Platt's Black'. This latter has very dark foliage and requires care in the choice of plants to grow with it. It shows to best effect when paired with something light and bright, such as *Carex testacea* or *C. albula*.

If one of the larger grasses such as *Chionochloa conspicua* or *C. flavicans* is used, a low ground-cover can help to emphasise the height of the grass, but there is also no reason why a taller ground-cover should not be used.

A to Z of native grasses

ANEMANTHELE
Gramineae

A genus of but one species which is confined to New Zealand. It was formerly known as *Stipa arundinacea*, *Oryzopsis rigida* and *O. lessoniana*. In some nurseries and garden centres it is still encountered as *O. rigida* or *O. lessoniana*.

Anemanthele lessoniana
Wind grass, gossamer grass

A medium-sized grass which forms bold clumps, up to 80 cm tall and 1 m across, of flowing or drooping stems and foliage. When grown in open situations the foliage has a yellowish to golden brown colour, but in shade, such as under trees, it is usually green. Its flowering stems are very graceful and give the plant a very light, feathery appearance. As the tiny spikelets come into flower they become a beautiful rosy red. When viewed against the light the whole plant then appears to shimmer with a light crimson haze or halo. After rain or heavy dew, wind grass is transformed into an object of great beauty because a myriad of small droplets of water cling to every part.

This is a most useful grass which can be used as a single specimen, for group planting to create a bold effect and as a ground-cover. Being a forest grass, it is ideal as a ground-cover under the light shade of trees, in those awkward places where few other plants will succeed. It is equally happy in open situations and, once established, is surprisingly drought tolerant. It is useful for dry banks and similar situations but it will not tolerate exposure to persistent salt-laden winds.

The flowering stems remain attractive for a few weeks, after which they should be removed before too many of the seeds ripen and have a chance to be scattered around. Its one fault is its propensity for self-sown seedlings to appear around the parent plant. The old flowering stems pull free quite easily, particularly if the open fingers of the hand are used to comb through the clumps. Burn or otherwise dispose of the stems in a safe manner, but do not put them in the compost bin.

In the United Kingdom two cultivars have been selected and are grown: 'Autumn Tints', in which the leaves are said to be flushed red in late summer, and 'Gold Hue', with leaves flushed golden yellow in late summer. In this country *Anemanthele* does not appear to show any marked variation and, as yet, no cultivars have been selected.

Propagation is usually from seed, which germinates very readily. If necessary, plants can be divided. It is hardy in lowland districts throughout New Zealand.

DESCRIPTION: Rather densely tufted, 60–80 cm tall. The leafy stems more or less erect, becoming wider spreading with age. Leaves 15–45 cm x 3–6 mm, flat, drooping, upper surface green to more or less glaucous and dull, under surface green and shining, the blade twisted near the base so as to bring the under surface uppermost; tips long drawn out. Flowering stem 30–150 cm long, with a large, open, drooping panicle; flower spikelets minute, 2.5–3 mm long.

DISTRIBUTION: North and South Islands; mainly on the eastern sides of both islands to South Otago. Occurs sparingly in drier, light, open bush or sometimes on rocky bluffs, but is not common.

AUSTROFESTUCA
Gramineae

From the Latin *australis*, southern, and *Festuca*, a genus of grasses.

A genus of one species, formerly included in *Festuca*. It is an Australasian plant found around the coastal areas of Australia and New Zealand.

Austrofestuca littoralis
Sand tussock

This species has a stiff, erect habit and forms pale, yellow-green or tawny tussocks up to 60 cm or so high. Its leaves have a coarse feel about them and are so strongly inrolled that they appear to be cylindrical. It is a coastal plant, growing in sandy or rocky places near the shore. It will stand up well to these conditions, making it ideal for coastal gardens.

It is not difficult to cultivate, requiring only well-drained soil and an open situation. While it may not be as ornamental as some other grasses, it should at least withstand difficult coastal conditions better than some of the more ornamental species. Easily propagated by division or from seed. It is sometimes incorrectly sold under the name of *Poa litorosa*, a quite different plant from the Subantarctic Islands.

DESCRIPTION: Forming dense, hard, erect tussocks up to 60 cm high. Leaves 40–60 cm long, about 1 mm in diameter, very strongly inrolled and appearing to be cylindrical, tips sharply pointed. Flowering stems 45–90 cm long with a narrow, dense flower panicle at the top.

DISTRIBUTION: North, South, Stewart and Chatham Islands. Sand dunes and rocky places near the shore.

BAUMEA
Cyperaceae

A comemmorative name honouring a person by the name of Baum.

Perennial herbs with a tufted or creeping habit and leaves that may be flat, rush-like, four-angled or, in some species, reduced to basal sheathing bracts. One or two of the species have some ornamental value, but generally they are of more use for environmental plantings. They are plants of damp ground and swampy areas, and require a moist soil for best results. All can be propagated by division or raised from seed.

The genus contains about 30 species and extends from Madagascar to India, Japan and around the Pacific region including Australia and New Zealand. There are seven native species, of which two are confined to New Zealand.

Baumea articulata

A strong-growing, rush-like plant, 80–180 cm tall, with thick, creeping rhizomes. It can be distinguished from a rush by the narrow, upright flower panicles which are produced at the tips of the flowering stems.

It is attractive, having a dramatic appearance, and could be used for planting in the shallow water near the edge of a pond or in the damp soil around its margin, however its spreading habit would probably preclude it from being used in many such situations. Its main use is for environmental-type plantings, particularly for assisting with the treatment of waste water.

DESCRIPTION: A stout rush-like plant 80–180 cm tall with thick, spreading rhizomes. Leaves cylindrical, tips awl-shaped, sharp; enclosed with long, papery, light brown bracts. Flowering stems similar to and about as long as the leaves; flower panicle 12–30 cm long, lax, branchlets in bundles, spikelets deep red-brown.

DISTRIBUTION: North Island from North Cape southwards to about Taupo and Hawke's Bay. Occurs in swamps and around the margins of lakes, often growing in shallow water. Sea level to 360 m.

Baumea complanata

A tufted plant 50–90 cm tall. The narrow, flat leaves are iris-like, pale to medium green, smooth and somewhat shining. It is rather similar to *Machaerina sinclairii* and could be used for similar purposes but its leaves are much narrower than *M. sinclairii* and it is possibly a more elegant plant. As an ornamental it has much to commend it and could be quite popular once it becomes better known.

In the garden it prefers a moist soil and some light shade, although it will grow in an open situation which is not too exposed.

DESCRIPTION: Tufted and leafy, 50–90 cm tall. Leaves 4–8 mm wide, pale to medium green, flat with smooth margins, tip acute. Flowering stems about as long as the leaves, about 3 mm wide and flattened. Flower panicle 15–50 cm long, narrow and erect, branchlets in bundles, flexible; spikelets light red-brown.

DISTRIBUTION: North Island. Not common and found only north of about the lower Bay of Plenty and Te Awamutu. Grows in damp ground in manuka scrub.

Baumea juncea

This is a rush-like plant which, under good conditions, will grow up to 90 cm tall. In general appearance it is not too dissimilar to *Leptocarpus* and can be used for similar purposes. It is used in ornamental horticulture and also for environmental plantings.

DESCRIPTION: A creeping rush-like plant with a rhizome 3–7 mm in diameter. Leaves all reduced to light brown sheathing bracts. Stems usually in tufts along the rhizome, 30–90 cm tall, 1.5–2.5 mm in diameter, smooth and pale bluish green. Inflorescence 2.5–7 cm long, stiff and erect, not much branched; spikelets red-brown.

DISTRIBUTION: North Island, common from North Cape southwards to about the lower Bay of Plenty and Kawhia but rare and local further south. South Island, rare throughout. Occurs in lowland swamps, salt marshes, damp sand on lake margins and river estuaries. Sea level to 275 m.

Baumea rubiginosa

This is another rather strongly creeping species which may be too aggressive for ornamental plantings. It has a rush-like appearance and will grow up to about 90 cm tall. Its main use is for revegetation plantings in wetlands. The name 'rubiginosa' refers to the red-brown colour of its inflorescences.

DESCRIPTION: Rush-like plant with a creeping rhizome 2–4 mm in diameter. Lower leaves reduced to grey-brown sheaths, upper leaves 1–3, similar to the stems and arising from the bases of the stems. Stems 30–90 cm tall, 1–2.5 mm in diameter, rather soft and a light blue-green. Flower panicles 6–18 cm long, branchlets in distant bundles, spikelets red-brown.

DISTRIBUTION: North Island, common throughout. South Island in Nelson, Westland and Southland less common, rare in Marlborough and Canterbury, Stewart and Chatham Islands. Usually in swampy places and lake margins. Sea level to 900 m.

Baumea teretifolia

A wide-spreading species which grows up to 1 m tall. It has rather thick rhizomes, and its yellow-green stems are cylindrical or slightly compressed. This plant is too vigorous for ornamental use but is ideal for planting to assist with the treatment of effluent.

DESCRIPTION: Densely tufted or covering large areas of ground. Rhizomes 2–4 mm in diameter, often far creeping. Stems 30–90 cm or more tall, 2–3 mm in diameter. Lowermost leaves reduced to sheathing bracts, upper leaves 1–3, shorter than or more or less equalling the stems. Flower panicle 4–18 cm long, stiff, erect, narrowed and pointed towards the tip.

DISTRIBUTION: North Island, from North Cape throughout but south of about Wanganui and Waipukurau only near Wellington. South Island, Nelson and Marlborough only. Lowland swamps and pakihi.

BOLBOSCHOENUS
Cyperaceae

From the Greek *bolbos*, a bulb, and *schoinos*, a rush, referring to the tuberous and swollen bases of its stems.

A small genus of grass-like herbs with three-angled stems tuberous and swollen at their bases. The leaves are grass-like, thin and usually longer than the stems. The inflorescence is terminal, with large leaf-like bracts arising from just below its base. The species occur in eastern Asia, north eastern America, New Zealand and Australia.

While they can be propagated from seed, division is the easiest and most convenient method.

Bolboschoenus fluviatilis
Ririwaka

The foliage of this plant resembles that of a *Carex* but it is easily distinguished because of the bulbous or tuberous bases of the stems. It is quite tall growing with thick, creeping rhizomes and can attain 1.5–2 m when in flower. The double-folded leaves are up to about 50 cm long, 7–11 mm wide.

It is a summer-green plant, dying down in the winter, and does not have any ornamental value. However, it is a good plant to use for assisting with the treatment of waste water. It was formerly used by Maori for thatching.

DESCRIPTION: A summer-green herb with thick, creeping rhizomes 7–9 mm in diameter. Leaves about 50 cm x 7–11 mm, double-folded but becoming flattened and grass-like, smooth. Flowering stems 1.5–2 m tall and three-angled; inflorescence terminal, a compound irregular umbel; spikelets dull red-brown.

DISTRIBUTION: North Island, from Northland to about Kawhia and the lower Bay of Plenty and then scattered to about Foxton and Napier. Grows in fresh water and brackish swamps, and river margins, usually never far from the coast.

CAREX
Cyperaceae

From the Greek *keiro*, to cut, alluding to the sharp cutting edges of the leaves.

Commonly known as sedge, *Carex* is a large genus of grass-like plants which provides us with some handsome and very useful garden subjects. Not only are some of the species most attractive, but carexes are very adaptable in the garden. Mostly, the cultivated species form dense tussocks which have fine, very attractive foliage in interesting shades and tones of bronze, copper, orange, bronzy pink and reddish colours, as well as the usual greens. In addition there are some which are lower growing and have a creeping habit.

The genus contains plants of great diversity of form and use. The various species can be used for ground-cover, as specimen plants, a back-drop for other plants or as a foil for bolder plants with different-coloured foliage. They are also ideal for creating a strong visual impact.

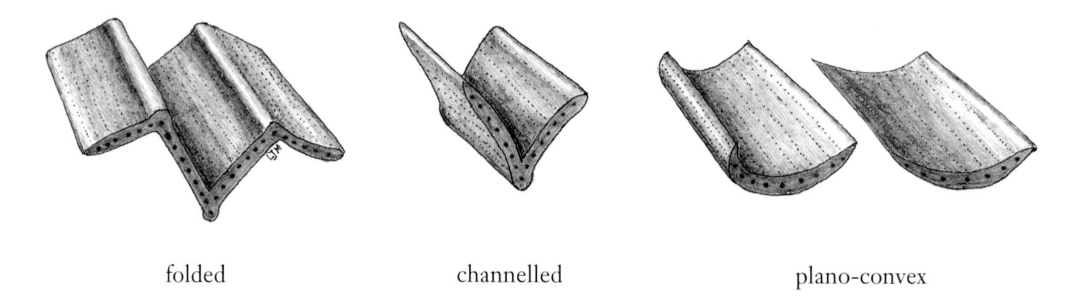

The different leaf profiles of carexes.

Many sedges inhabit damp ground in grasslands, swamps, bogs, forests or in scrub. While they will readily adapt to similar conditions in the garden, it must not be thought that those are the only conditions under which they will grow. Nothing could be further from the truth, because some will grow readily in ordinary garden soils and others will even tolerate very dry conditions once well established.

In New Zealand the genus contains more than 70 species, while world-wide it contains more than a thousand, mainly found in temperate and colder regions. Those species with sharp, cutting edges on their leaves are generally referred to as 'cutty-grasses'. Sedges can be distinguished from true grasses by their stems being solid inside, often triangular in section, and their leaves being in three vertical rows and usually arising from the base of the plant only.

Propagation is commonly from seed, but most species can also be divided. Division is the best, or only, way of propagating selected clones and for some cultivars, although *C. comans* 'Frosted Curls' does come reasonably true from seed.

Carex albula

A most striking and useful sedge, 30–45 cm tall, usually a pale buff colour or almost white. It has a tufted to erect-tufted habit and is a most useful plant for the garden, where it can be grown by itself or in association with darker-foliaged plants which would emphasise its light colouring. Particularly during the colder months of the year, its appearance can become very white.

Carex albula is not yet well known in cultivation and is sometimes confused with *C. comans* 'Frosted Curls'. This latter plant never becomes as white as *C. albula* and is also distinguished by its lower habit of growth and sprawling mop-head of foliage. Once *C. albula* becomes better known it could become more popular than *C. comans* 'Frosted Curls' and there should be a place for it in most gardens.

DESCRIPTION: A tufted plant 25–45 cm tall, pale buff to almost white in colour. Leaves 25–50 cm long, 1–1.5 mm wide, flattened to very slightly channelled, margins rough to the touch, tips only slightly curled. Flowering stems much shorter than the leaves; flower spikes 3–6, terminal one male, female spikes 0.5–2 cm x 3–5 mm.

DISTRIBUTION: South Island, where it is found in the MacKenzie Country, North Otago, near Kurow and at Hyde. 200–750 m.

Carex berggrenii

A small species forming small to broad tufts or patches of bronze or dull red foliage. It is easily recognised by its almost flat leaves with broad, blunt tips.

This species is quite attractive when well grown but is, perhaps, more of a plant for rock-garden or native-plant enthusiasts. It would be quite useful for growing in a trough garden where its low, grassy foliage, compact growth and bronze colour could be used as a contrast against plants with broader foliage. It requires a moist or damp soil and will not withstand dry conditions.

DESCRIPTION: Shortly creeping to form small patches. Leaves 3–6 cm long by 1–2.5 mm wide. The short flower spikelets are usually produced in threes and set down among the leaves. Stems enclosed by light brown leaf-sheaths.

DISTRIBUTION: Occurs throughout much of the South Island, in boggy ground, damp river flats and around lake shores. Rare outside of Canterbury and Otago. 300–1500 m.

Carex buchananii

The whole plant has a reddish brown colour and generally has a rather stiff and erect habit. In addition to its growth habit, it is usually recognised by the fine tips of the leaves being bleached and very distinctively curled.

This is one of the best species for use in the garden on account of its coloration and stiff habit, which provides a very effective contrast when grown with other plants, as opposed to the flowing habits of other grasses. It also associates well with the formal lines of modern architecture. On younger plants the stiff leaves spread only slightly outwards from a densely tufted base, but as the plants age the leaves become much more widely spreading.

DESCRIPTION: A rather densely tufted species 50–75 cm tall with a stiff and rather erect habit. Leaves to 60 cm or more long, about 2–2.5 mm wide, flattened to slightly channelled but often rolled to appear cylindrical. Flowering stems about as long as or slightly shorter than the leaves; flower-spikes 5–6, silvery; the uppermost spike (or 2 spikes) male, lower spikes female, 0.5–3 cm x 3–4 mm.

DISTRIBUTION: North and South Islands. Occurs only in the lower half of the North Island and is quite local. It is more widely distributed in the South Island, being locally common down the eastern side but rare in Southland. Not recorded from Westland and Fiordland.

Carex chathamica

This is a rather bold species which is useful for growing in moist soils. It is somewhat similar to, but smaller than, *C.trifida* and grows 35–45 cm tall. It prefers to be grown in an open situation and its light green foliage associates well with golden-foliaged plants, particularly those with broad leaves. It is one of the carexes which are distinguished by having quite large and prominent flower-spikes.

DESCRIPTION: A stout, rather rigid plant about 35–45 cm tall. Leaves light green, double-folded and 6–10 mm wide with long, tapering tips; the densely and minutely toothed margins have sharp cutting edges, particularly along the upper half. Flowering stems triangular in section and up to 35 cm tall; flowering spikes erect, brown, up to 7.5 x 1.5 cm. and quite prominent.

DISTRIBUTION: Confined to the Chatham Islands, where it grows in peaty and swampy ground in open situations.

Carex cirrhosa

A small tufted sedge to 25 cm high, usually a grey- or bronze-green but occasionally may be reddish. One of its distinguishing characters is the very distinctively curled and twisted tips of the leaves.

Unless a really good coloured form can be found, this species has only limited appeal. The most attractive feature of the currently cultivated form is the curly leaf tips, which are quite interesting. Being a plant of moist places, it could be useful for growing in damp soils in open situations. Several plants grouped together would provide a better effect than just one plant by itself.

DESCRIPTION: A small, densely tufted, grey-green or reddish plant 20–25 cm tall. Leaves no more than 1 mm wide and very distinctively curled and twisted at the tips when dry; the dry tips are usually a pale brownish colour. The flowering stems are usually much shorter than the leaves and more or less hidden among them.

DISTRIBUTION: North Island from Lake Waikaremoana to Kaweka Lakes and Lake Wairarapa. South Island in scattered localities from North Canterbury to about Lake Tekapo. Usually on the margins of lakes, ponds and in river-beds. 600–1000 m, but occasionally lowland.

Carex comans

A densely tufted and very leafy species, usually no more than 30–40 cm tall. In the garden it has a long, flowing habit of growth with the leaves spreading out over the ground for quite some distance. In the wild the leaves are quite frequently shorter and more erect, giving the plant a rather different appearance. The colour of the foliage varies from reddish to a brownish grey or to a pale green. As with some other species, the ends of the leaves become bleached. They are also slightly curled but not as conspicuously as with *C. buchananii*. When first produced, the flowering stems are 25 to perhaps 40 cm long, but as the seeds ripen they elongate and lie along the ground, eventually becoming up to 1–1.3 m in length. Along with the foliage they form a not unattractive, rather tangled mass. For obvious reasons, British gardeners refer to this and similar species as mop-headed sedges.

In the nursery trade considerable confusion surrounds this species, and some plants being sold as *C. comans* are not that species at all.

C. comans grows easily in most soils and will tolerate quite a wide range of conditions. It will grow in shady (not overhead) situations but is really better out in the sun. It is also quite tolerant of coastal conditions. Once established it will withstand considerable dryness.

Being of lower growth it is most useful along the front of a border or in front of other plantings where it is desired to create a contrast. When planting in groups, plants should be given sufficient space to allow for their flowing habit. Once a year it should be groomed to remove any dead foliage and the old flowering stems. The latter pull free very easily. Some of the brownish forms of *C. comans* tend to be dull and dingy and lack the brightness of some other forms of this species and of other species. Perhaps it is time for some discerning plant collector to bring into cultivation a better-coloured form.

DESCRIPTION: Densely tufted and very leafy, reddish to greyish brown or light green, 30–40 cm tall. Leaves 25–40 cm or more long, usually 1–1.5 mm wide, tips distinctively curled. Flowering stems 25–40 cm long, at maturity greatly elongating and lying along the ground; flower-spikes 5–7, 5 mm–2.5cm x 3–4 mm.

DISTRIBUTION: Found throughout New Zealand, except for Fiordland. It occurs in damp pasture, damp places in tussock grassland, on river flats and along the sides of tracks through forests. In Southland it is variously known as Longwood tussock and Tokanui tussock.

Carex comans 'Bronze'

Differs in being a warm, almost pinkish, bronze colour, which is more lively than some of the dull brownish forms of this species. The effect is heightened by some of the younger leaves having a distinctly pinkish colour and by the light green of the young leaves, which shows at the base of the clump. It is a very effective plant, especially with blue-grey grasses and plants with silver leaves.

Some plants sold under this name appear to be forms of *C. flagellifera*, and can be distinguished by their taller, more erect habit of growth and the tips of the leaves not having the distinctive curl of *C. comans.*

Carex comans 'Frosted Curls'

This selection is distinguished by having very pale green foliage which, with its bleached ends, gives the whole plant a very whitish appearance. It is most effective in the garden because its distinct colouring allows for some interesting planting combinations. It is sometimes sold simply as *C. comans*; however, as the species comprises a number of different colour forms, the cultivar name should always be used when referring to this particular form.

It was discovered at Cape Egmont and brought into cultivation in 1975 by Terry Hatch of Joy Plants, Pukekohe. It was given its cultivar name because frosted hair-styles were the vogue with women at that time. According to Mr Hatch, much of what is now being grown as 'Frosted Curls' is simply wild collected forms of *C. comans* which are being wrongly cultivated as 'Frosted Curls'. The true 'Frosted Curls' is quite soft to the touch, whereas other similar plants are coarser and harsher.

It is sometimes erroneously sold under the name of *Carex albula* 'Frosted Curls'. *Carex albula* is a distinct species which has more erect growth, does not have the curled tips to the leaves and the whole plant becomes conspicuously whitened, particularly during the colder months of the year.

Carex devia

An as yet little-known but very distinct and interesting sedge. It has tufts of quite stiff, erect foliage and grows to about 30 cm or so tall. If it is in a moist, more shaded situation, its foliage is green; if in an open situation and dry conditions, it can be a mixture of green and gold. After flowering the maturing flowering stems elongate and droop over until they are 60 cm or more long.

Its smaller size makes it suitable for smaller gardens. It grows best in a reasonably moist soil but, once established, will tolerate quite dry conditions.

DESCRIPTION: Tufts sometimes rather loose, green or yellow-green, up to 30 cm tall. Leaves stiff and erect, up to 38 cm long, 2–3 mm wide, deeply channelled. Flowering stems 15–25 cm long, at first erect, but as the seeds mature it elongates and droops until it becomes up to 75 cm long. Flower spikes 2–4, 2.5–4 cm long, 3–4 mm in diameter. Terminal spike (or two spikes) male, 3–4 cm long, 2–3 mm in diameter.

DISTRIBUTION: South Island, confined to serpentine areas in Nelson Province. Usually occurs in boggy openings in forest and scrub, on stream-banks and on serpentine scree. 300–1170 m.

Carex dipsacea

Carex dipsacea resembles *C. flagellifera* and *C. testacea* in both habit and its channelled leaves but differs mainly in details of its seeds. Cultivated forms of this species appear to have a more erect habit.

The usually grown form of *C. dipsacea* is light green, and where a contrast or foliage colour, other than the more highly coloured sedges, is required it is a useful plant. Its densely tufted habit is also handy when using it in the garden, especially in association with grasses of a more flowing habit. Its light green colour should be tried in conjunction with red- and purple-foliaged plants. An underplanting of a purple-foliaged *Acaena* would be very effective.

DESCRIPTION: A densely tufted species 30–75 cm tall with light green or reddish leaves which are quite harsh to the touch. The leaves are channelled, narrow (1.5–2.5 mm wide) and on young plants, at least, are stiff and erect. The flowering stems are usually shorter than the the leaves.

DISTRIBUTION: North and South Islands. Usually occurs on the margins of swamps, in boggy river flats, tussock grassland or in damp places in forest. Sea level to 1200 m.

Carex dissita

The bright, fresh green, graceful foliage makes this an attractive species which is useful for associating with bolder-foliaged plants, particularly those with yellow or yellow-variegated foliage. It can also be used with *Festuca coxii*. Although the leaf colour of *C. dissita* can vary from green to reddish, only the green form appears to be in cultivation. The almost black seed-spikes are a feature of this species and make it well worth growing. They also help to distinguish it from similar species.

Being mainly a forest and scrub dweller, it is very suitable for planting in shaded situations, such as a ground-cover under trees or shrubs, or on the shady side of a fence or building. It should preferably be grown in a moist soil.

DESCRIPTION: Forms bright green or reddish clumps 45–80 cm tall. Leaves arching outwards, 1.5–6 mm wide, double-folded, midrib dark, especially in the lower half of the leaf, margins finely scabrid. Flowering stems shorter than the leaves; flower-spikes 0.5–2.5 cm long by 4–6 mm wide, mostly female with a few male flowers at the base of each, usually very dark coloured.

DISTRIBUTION: Occurs throughout the North, South and Stewart Islands, in forest, scrub and swampy ground. Sea level to 1200 m.

Carex elingamita

This is a robust sedge which will grow to about 1 m or so tall. Apart from its size and the distinctive leaf-like bracts on its flower-stems, this species does not have a great deal to commend it as a garden plant. Its height possibly gives it some value as a background plant where its light green foliage would act as a foil for other plants, or it could be featured with a low, carpeting plant, such as *Leptinella calcarea* or *Pratia angulata*. While this species is confined to the Three Kings Island, reports indicate that it may tolerate more frost than might be expected. It is probably mainly of interest to collectors rather than the average gardener. Its common name commemorates the wreck of the S.S. *Elingamite* in 1902.

DESCRIPTION: A tall, clump-forming sedge growing to about 1 m when in flower. The double-folded leaves are shorter than the flowering stems, up to 1 cm or so wide, have finely scabrid (rough to the touch) margins and are a light green colour. There are about 10 erect flower-spikes on each flowering stem, and the lowermost spikes arise from long leaf-like bracts which hang down and are distinctively curled and twisted.

DISTRIBUTION: Only on the Three Kings Islands, where it was discovered in 1889.

Carex flagellifera

In general appearance, *Carex flagellifera* is rather similar to *C. testacea* and *C. comans*, differing mainly in its colour, although it is usually taller and less sprawling than *C. comans*. It can be used for much the same purposes as those two species but is probably better when grown in slightly moister soils. It appears to be one of the most commonly used species but suffers very much from the fact that, all too often, poorly coloured forms are used. The worst forms of this species are a dingy, greyish bronze, giving the plant a cold and lifeless appearance. The plain green and bronze forms are better, and there is also a very good form with purplish red foliage. The young leaves of this last form often show some pinkish colour, which gives the plant a much warmer and more lively appearance.

A brownish bronze form of *C. flagellifera* not infrequently appears in nurseries and garden centres under the name of *C. lucida*, a name which is regarded as being synonymous with *C. flagellifera*. Sometimes it is also sold as *C. comans* or *C. comans*

'Bronze', both of which are incorrect.

The greatly elongated fruiting stems of both *C. flagellifera* and *C. testacea* have, for obvious reasons, earned them the common name of 'trip-me-up'.

DESCRIPTION: A variable species which has dense tufts of arching leaves to form a mop-head. Its colour varies from a shining green to bronze or brownish to purplish red. The channelled leaves are 1.5–2.5 mm wide and are sharply scabrid along their margins. The flowering stems are 35–75 cm when first produced, but as the seeds mature they often elongate to 2 m or so and lie along the ground.

DISTRIBUTION: Found in the Kermadec, North, South and Stewart Islands. Grows in damp areas or around forest margins from sea level to 1100 m.

Carex flagellifera 'Bronze Delight'

A selection which has warm brownish or bronze foliage. It is an attractive cultivar which originated in Oaklands Nursery, Motueka, in 1996.

Carex gaudichaudiana

A densely tufted sedge with a creeping rhizome, ultimately forming a wider-spreading plant up to 30 cm or more tall. Its soft, green leaves are narrow and double-folded. Their dried tips are usually twisted or curled. It requires a moist soil and will grow in an open situation providing it has sufficient moisture. Although usually grown as an ornamental, it is basically a plant of grassy appearance and does not really have a great deal to commend it.

DESCRIPTION: A densely tufted plant with a creeping rhizome, sometimes long creeping. Leaves soft, 20–30 cm or more long, up to 3 mm wide, double-folded, the dried tips twisted. Flowering stems 6–32 cm long and three-angled; flower-spikes 3–5, usually sessile, 0.5–1.5 cm or more long, 2.5 mm in diameter.

DISTRIBUTION: North Island, scattered throughout and common in the Waikato. South Island, occurs throughout. Usually in boggy ground. Sea level to 1800 m.

Carex geminata

Cutty grass

With its wide-spreading habit, this is not the kind of plant that one would wish to plant in a garden, and it is useful for environmental planting, such as creating or restoring a wetland area, providing a wildlife habitat or assisting with waste-water treatment.

DESCRIPTION: A strongly growing species usually 50–100 cm. It has creeping rhizomes and forms quite large patches or colonies. Medium green leaves double-folded, 5–9 mm wide, 75–120 cm long and much longer than the flowering stems.

DISTRIBUTION: North Island from near Dargaville southwards. Throughout the South Island but lesss common on the eastern side. Stewart Island. In damp or swampy ground. Sea level to 600 m.

Carex 'Goldilocks'

A very fine plant and a distinct break from most other carexes. *Carex* 'Goldilocks' associates very well with any grasses or other plants with blue-grey foliage. It is also an ideal companion for the golden brown form of *C. testacea*, each complementing the other very nicely. An under-planting of one of the green-leaved species of *Leptinella* would be a most effective way of showing this cultivar to great advantage.

It originated as a chance seedling, in Nikau Gardens Nursery, Nelson. *Carex buchananii* is one parent and it is believed that *C. comans* is probably the other. Its erect habit of growth and the distinctively curled leaf-tips betray its *C. buchananii* parentage. Propagate by division.

DESCRIPTION: A densely tufted, upright plant, 70–80 cm or so tall. Foliage a very attractive golden colour usually with underlying shades of a bronzy green; tips of the leaves distinctively curled. Flowering stems lie on the ground and are considerably longer than the leaves, up to 1.5 m in length. At first its habit is fairly stiff and erect, but with age the leaves tend to spread outwards in a rather graceful manner.

Carex 'Greenie'

This cultivar is like a larger form of *C. comans* but its yellow-green colour is quite distinct. Being of relatively low habit it is useful for growing in front of taller grasses and other plants, while its wide-spreading foliage is good for covering quite large areas. It will tolerate relatively dry conditions but is much better if it has adequate moisture most of the time.

This is another hybrid which originated in Nikau Gardens Nursery, Nelson. It has *C. comans* (probably 'Frosted Curls') as one parent, and the curled leaf tips indicate that *C. buchananii* could be the other. Propagate by division only.

DESCRIPTION: A fairly large mop-headed sedge growing to about 30 cm or so tall and spreading out over the ground to cover an area about 1–1.2 m across. Long, flowing foliage is a yellowish green; narrow leaves are channelled and 1–1.5 mm wide, distinctively curled at their tips. Flowering stems elongate as the seeds mature to lie on the ground in an interesting, tangled mass; when mature they may be up to 2 m or more in length.

Carex inopinata

In some respects this is rather like a smaller version of *C. wakatipu*, except that it forms wider-spreading patches rather than the tighter clumps of that species. It is seldom more than about 5 cm tall. As a plant it is probably of more interest to specialists and rock-garden enthusiasts than the average gardener. It could be useful if contrasted with low-growing plants of differing foliage.

DESCRIPTION: A small, creeping species with narrow, grass-like leaves up to 10 cm long. Leaves spreading, up to 2 mm wide, channelled, bright green above and paler beneath. Flowering stems much shorter than the leaves and usually with three short flower-spikes.

DISTRIBUTION: Confined to the South Island where it occurs in the Broken River basin and near Bendigo in Central Otago. It grows among limestone rocks and in rock debris.

Carex kermadecensis

A rather strong-growing plant of arching habit, to 50 cm or more tall, with broad, double-folded leaves of bright green. It forms quite attractive tufts and is useful for growing in light shade. Providing it is not too exposed, it can also be grown in a more open situation. A reasonably moist soil is preferable if good growth is to be obtained. It is hardy to light and possibly moderate frosts.

DESCRIPTION: A robust plant forming dense tufts up to 50 cm or more tall. Leaves 60 cm or more long, 7–10 mm wide, bright green, double-folded, margins have rough edges. Flowering stems up to 45 cm tall, three-angled, much shorter than the leaves; flower-spikes 2–5.5 cm long, 5–7 mm in diameter, erect on stiff stalks.

DISTRIBUTION: Kermadec Islands, where it is common on Sunday Island.

Carex lambertiana

This species is very similar to *C. dissita* but is a more robust plant. It will grow into quite large clumps up to 60 cm or so high. At least two forms of it are in cultivation—one with leaves about 6 mm wide and the other with much narrower leaves. Apart from the leaf width, both appear to be rather similar.

While it can be grown in an open situation, it is probably best grown in indirect shade or under the light, overhead shade of trees. Apart from its larger size, there is not enough difference between this and *C. dissita* to warrant growing both. However, where a larger plant is required, *C. lambertiana* could be the one to grow.

DESCRIPTION: Forming quite large, spreading tufts from 60 cm to 1 m tall. Leaves double-folded, bright green or yellow-green, 3–6 mm wide and usually rather rough to the touch. Flowering stems about the same length as the leaves; flower-spikes about 5 cm x 5 mm, dark reddish brown.

DISTRIBUTION: North and South Islands as far south as Banks Peninsula. Common in the northern part of the North Island, but less common and more scattered from there south. Grows in lowland forest, scrub and swamps, usually not far from the coast.

Carex lessoniana

This species is closely related to *C. geminata* and is a robust plant growing up to 1 m or more tall. It is used for very much the same purposes as *C. geminata* and, because of its strongly spreading rhizomes, is excellent for holding stream-banks to protect them from erosion.

DESCRIPTION: Differs from *C. geminata* only in one or two minute botanical details relating to its seeds.

DISTRIBUTION: North Island, throughout except along the eastern side. South Island, southwards to about Kekerengu on the east and Charleston on the west, and rare further south. Occurs in lowland peat swamps. To 600 m.

Carex maorica

This species is probably of more use for environmental and regeneration plantings than in the garden, although it possibly could have some value for planting in wet soils.

DESCRIPTION: Forms light green, upright, arching tufts or clumps 50–100 cm tall. Leaves double-folded, 5–7 mm wide, up to 1 m long, they are quite rough along the margins. Seeds on the flower-spike widely spreading, giving it a very distinctive appearance.

DISTRIBUTION: Occurs in lowland swamps throughout most of the North and South Islands.

Carex petriei

An erect or loosely spreading plant up to about 35 cm tall and usually a red or brownish red colour. Characters by which it may be distinguished are the broad, sheathing bases of the leaves and their fine, curled and twisted tips. It has been likened to a smaller *C. buchananii* of a somewhat weaker and pinker hue. However, as it is known in New Zealand, it is definitely more strongly red than *C. buchananii*, and not a weaker pink.

This is a most handsome and colourful species which, unfortunately, is rather scarce in cultivation. What purports to be this species appears to be either a form of *C. buchananii* or perhaps a hybrid of that species. A brownish form of *C. comans* is occasionally also sold as *C. petriei*. It requires a moist soil in an open situation to obtain the best from it. Being a medium-sized plant, it creates a better effect if several are planted as a group. It would look well when grown in a suitable contrasting mat plant such as the green form of *Leptinella calcarea*.

DESCRIPTION: Densely tufted, 20–35 cm tall, erect to loosely spreading, red or brownish red. Leaves 1–2 mm wide, slightly channelled, pink or greenish red, tips curled and twisted when dry, broad sheathing bases about three times the width of the blade. Flower-stems usually slightly longer than the leaves; flower-spikes 3–6, dark red-brown, 1–3 cm long x 3–6 mm wide.

DISTRIBUTION: North Island, Kaimanawa Mountains. South Island, southwards to about Otago but absent from Westland. Not particularly common. Occurs on stream-banks, river-flats or in tussock grassland, in moist or swampy places. 700–1500 m.

Carex resectans

This is quite a small species which is really more suited to growing in a rock garden or a trough garden. However, as it can form turfy patches, it could be grown right at the front of a border. It is another species which is of possibly more interest to the collector or native-plant enthusiast. It is a plant of dry soils and sandy areas near the coast. In some parts of its range, notably Central and North Otago, it has become a weed in some pasture lands and lucerne crops.

DESCRIPTION: A small, slowly creeping species, usually no more than than 4–6 cm high and forming dense, circular patches. Leaves erect, up to 8 cm long by about 1 mm wide, shining green and almost flattened. Flowering stems shorter than the leaves and almost hidden among them; flower-spikes forming a compact head up to 1 cm long and set among 2–3 leaf-like bracts.

DISTRIBUTION: North Island, near Wellington at Manurewa Point and near Cape Palliser. South Island, on the eastern side from Marlborough to North and Central Otago. Usually on sand in coastal areas, inland in low tussock grassland, or in dry, depleted pasture. Sea level to alpine regions.

Carex secta

Purei

This is a well-known species which is quite commonly seen in swampy and boggy ground, where its large, flowing tussocks usually rise above the swamp on trunks formed from their own tightly matted roots. It is a most handsome sedge but is too common to be properly appreciated.

It is actually a most attractive plant and is seen at its best when planted on the edge of a water feature such as a pond or lake, or even a stream. While it does not have to be grown alongside water and will grow in a soil which remains constantly moist, there is no doubt that it is seen to best advantage beside water. When grown in open situations it takes on an attractive yellow-green or slightly golden hue, with the colour becoming intensified during the winter months. If grown in less exposed or shadier conditions, the foliage is usually green.

C. secta is also a most useful plant for use in re-establishing or enhancing wetland areas. The early English colonists always knew *C. secta* as 'nigger-head' and never by any other name. Such a name is now regarded as politically incorrect and has been abandoned. It has therefore been necessary take up one of its several Maori common names and use that instead.

DESCRIPTION: Large tussocks often forming thick trunks, up to 1 m tall, from its densely matted roots and old stem-bases. Leaves drooping, up to about 90 cm or more long, 3–7 mm wide, slightly channelled above. Flowering stems about as long as the leaves or slightly shorter, three-angled. Flower spikelets numerous, pale brown, clustered towards the ends of slender branchlets.

DISTRIBUTION: North, South and Stewart Islands. Usually common in swamps throughout. Sea level to 900 m.

Carex solandri

A tufted sedge about 50–60 cm tall with green or yellow-green, drooping foliage of attractive appearance. Being mainly a forest plant, it is happier in a shaded situation, although it will grow reasonably well in a more open location. It is a useful plant for growing under the shade of trees where it may be difficult to establish other plants. While it prefers a moist soil, it will tolerate quite dry conditions for limited periods.

DESCRIPTION: Forming dense tufts up to 60 cm or more tall. Leaves drooping, 3–6.5 mm wide, double-folded, green to yellow-green. Flowering stems as long as, or longer than, the leaves, three-angled; flower-spikes 5–10, 1–4.5 cm long, nodding on long, slender stalks.

DISTRIBUTION: North Island, common throughout but more so on the eastern side. South Island, throughout most of the island but rare or absent from Fiordland and Southland. Stewart Island. Usually in forest but also in damp ground, particularly on river flats. Sea level to 600 m.

Carex tenuiculmis

This species was, until recently, known as *C. secta* var. *tenuiculmis*. It is similar to, but differs from, the typical form in its slightly smaller size, more slender flowering stems and narrower leaves. The foliage of the cultivated form is distinctly brownish or bronze, and that is what makes it such an appealing plant for gardeners. One author describes it as being a glowing, deep warm brown colour. This is a very fine plant and worthy of a place in any garden where a suitable position is available.

DISTRIBUTION: South Island, mainly in inland Canterbury, and rare in Nelson and Otago. Stewart and Chatham Islands. Sea level to 650 m.

Carex testacea

In habit this species somewhat resembles *C. dipsacea* but is wider spreading, not as tall and differs mainly in several botanical details relating to the seeds. *C. dipsacea* rarely ever assumes the rich coloration of *C. testacea*.

While the colour of *C. testacea* is rather variable, what is probably the most commonly grown form becomes a rich golden-brown or orange when grown in an open situation. It is particularly handsome at all times of the year, and if the very long flowering stems become a nuisance, it is a simple matter to groom the plant and remove them. It combines well with silver- or grey-foliaged plants, as well as plants with bold foliage. In the garden it is very hardy, withstanding dry conditions very well, and it is also useful for growing in coastal gardens.

DESCRIPTION: A densely tufted plant, 50–60 cm tall, with arching, rather wide-spreading foliage. Colour varies from green to a light brownish green or golden brown. Narrow, channelled leaves usually about 2 mm wide. When flowering stems first appear they are about the same length as the leaves, but after flowering elongate as the seeds mature; eventually they may be up to 2 m or more in length and sprawl over the ground.

DISTRIBUTION: Throughout both North and South Islands, where it occurs in lowland to montane forests, fescue tussock grasslands and on sand-dunes.

Carex trifida

Tataki

This is distinguished from other native species by its large size, stout habit, numerous large flower-spikes and its wide, medium to deep green leaves which are greyish on the back. It is a very handsome species which is well worth a place in the garden.

Its bold clumps of foliage are 60–80 cm or more tall, and in open situations the glaucous bloom on the leaves is most pronounced. When it flowers, the plump, brown flower-spikes add to its attractiveness. It should be grown in a moist soil, although I have seen it growing reasonably well on a dry bank. It is also a plant which will grow well in indirect shade such as on the south side of a fence or building.

Its common name originates from Stewart Island, where it is fairly common; the islanders generally refer to it as 'tataki grass'.

DESCRIPTION: A stout plant forming dense clumps or tussocks, 60–90 cm tall. Leaves 50–90 cm long, 6 mm–1.5 cm or more wide, in cross-section double-folded, upper surface medium to dark green, under surface glaucous. Flowering stems 15–90 cm tall, rigid, slightly three-angled; flower-spikes 6–9 or sometimes more, brown to greyish brown, 3.5–11 cm long, 5 mm–1.5 cm in diameter.

DISTRIBUTION: South Island in coastal regions from Stephens Island to Banks Peninsula and scattered localities south of North Otago. Stewart, Chatham, Snares, Auckland, Campbell and Macquarie Islands. Usually on coastal cliffs and rock outcrops or boggy shorelines. Also occurs in Chile, Fuegia and the Falkland Islands.

Carex ventosa

A very handsome and bold species which is closely related to *C. chathamica*, and it also resembles *C. trifida*. It has very handsome foliage, green above and slightly blue-grey beneath, while the flower-spikes are also a feature when they appear. Being a plant of mainly open situations, it grows well in full sun, but it can also be grown in light shade. While it does best in a moist soil, it also grows quite well in slightly drier situations.

DESCRIPTION: A large tufted sedge of flowing habit, up to 60 cm or more tall when in flower. Leaves may be 90–100 cm long not overtopping the flowering stems, double-folded, 1–1.7 cm wide, upper surface bright medium green, under surface greyish green or glaucous, margins slightly scabrid. Flower-spikes erect, up to 9.5 cm long by 6–8 mm in diameter.

DISTRIBUTION: Confined to the Chatham Islands. Grows in open forest or scrub, or in rocky places.

Carex virgata

This species is quite closely related to *C. secta* but does not attain the same size as that species. It forms a handsome, bright green tussock up to about 90 cm tall and with a graceful appearance. Initially it grows directly out of the ground, but older plants may grow trunks formed from their thickly matted roots.

Being a plant of swampy places, it is ideal for growing alongside water or in very damp soils. It can be used for the same purposes as *C. secta* and in some ways could be more useful because it does not grow quite as large. Its distinctively coloured foliage could be desirable either as a contrast with other plants or where the more golden colour of *C. secta* may not be suitable.

DESCRIPTION: A rather large, tussock-forming sedge with arching foliage, ultimately growing up to 1.2 m tall. Narrow leaves usually 2–5 mm wide, 50–120 cm long; they are quite distinct, having a dark midrib and darkish margins while the in-between areas are a pale whitish green.

DISTRIBUTION: Occurs in swampy places throughout the North, South, Stewart and Chatham Islands. Sea level to about 800 m.

Carex wakatipu

This is a rather variable species, with the more densely tufted forms usually having wider leaves than those slowly spreading forms which make slightly larger clumps. The only form which appears to be in cultivation has green leaves about 2 mm wide and forms reasonably compact tufts or clumps. It is a pleasant enough plant, although perhaps of more interest for growing in a rock garden or in a trough garden, where size is important. Alternatively, its tufted habit and bright green foliage could make it useful for the front of a border, where it could be associated with broader-leaved plants having yellow or pale-green foliage, or with silver or blue-grey foliage.

It would be interesting to obtain those forms which have reddish green and yellowish green foliage to ascertain whether they have more garden merit than the currently cultivated form.

DESCRIPTION: A rather variable species, being shortly rhizomatous to form larger clumps, or more densely tufted, with tufts 12–30 cm high, dark green, reddish green or yellowish green. Leaves 2–4 mm wide, erect or spreading, channelled and with a small but distinct keel on the under surface. Flowering stems either shorter than the leaves or sometimes elongating in fruit and becoming longer than the leaves.

DISTRIBUTION: Occurs in the South Island, where it is common in snow-tussock grassland and fescue-tussock grassland from 450–1700 m.

CHIONOCHLOA
Gramineae

From the Greek *chion*, snow, and *chloe*, grass, referring to their common name of 'snow grass'.

A predominantly New Zealand genus ranging from large tussock grasses to smaller tufted and sward-forming or creeping grasses which give our grasslands a very distinctive character. The taller species are often collectively known as snow grasses, while individually they are referred to as snow tussocks. The tallest may be up to 2 m but generally they average about 1 m tall. In the early days tramps or swaggers who roamed the back country looking for work were often referred to as 'tussockies', from their habit of tying together the tops of the tall tussocks to form a shelter when they bedded down at night. In such a shelter they would be quite snug and protected from strong winds.

Chionochloa provides the gardener with some truly magnificent grasses which have strong form and graceful flower-heads. They are bold enough to be used as individual specimens or they can be used most effectively for massed planting. The more commonly cultivated species are quite easy to grow and will do well in any reasonable soil. Most prefer a well-drained soil, while some, such as *C. rubra*, will tolerate somewhat moister conditions. When well established, some will cope with considerable dryness while other species require a more constantly moist soil.

Propagation is generally by seed; division can also be used, although it is better for young plants rather than old ones.

The various species occur in a wide range of habitats from coastal cliffs and bluffs to forest, scrub, well-drained to poorly drained grasslands, cushion bogs, snow hollows and ultramafic soils and rocks. They range from coastal Northland to the Subantarctic islands and are an important constituent of many of the grasslands in the central North Island and those east of the main divide in the South Island. Identification of the species is not always easy and usually relies on the form of the leaf and the nature of its sheathing base, such as whether it fractures into short or long segments, remains whole and still attached to the plant, or whether the old leaves remain attached to the plant instead of breaking off. The colour of the leaf-sheath can also be helpful with identification of some species.

There are 22 species native to New Zealand and one species confined to Australia. In addition some of the species are divided into a number of subspecies and forms.

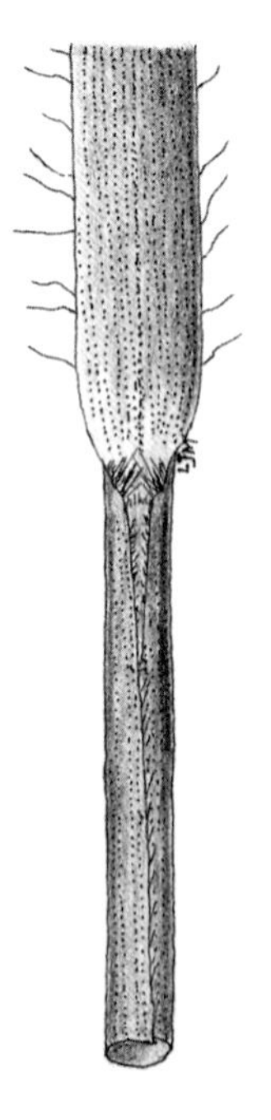

Chionochloa flavescens, detail of leaf-sheath and ligule.

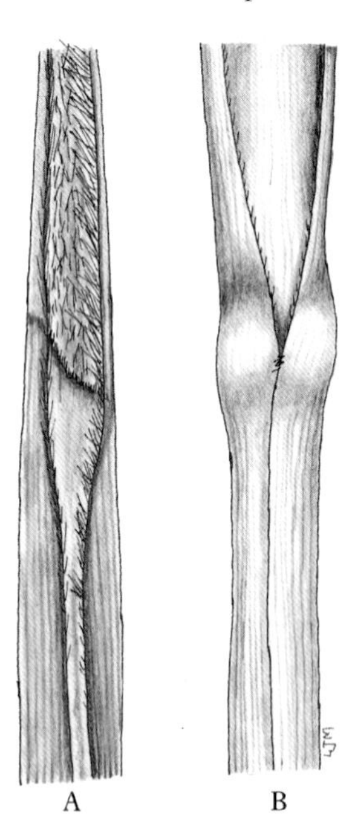

(A): *Chionochloa rubra* ssp. *cuprea*.
(B): *Chionochloa flavicans*, detail of leaf-sheath and ligule.

Chionochloa beddiei

An attractive tussock which somewhat resembles *C. flavicans* in general appearance. Its smaller size makes it more useful for gardens where space is limited, and it is also ideal for growing in a container. *C. beddiei* prefers a moderately moist, well-drained soil and should be grown in an open situation. Flowering is usually during October.

DESCRIPTION: Forms a smaller tussock, up to about 60 cm tall, which has rather widely spreading leaves. Leaves 30–60 cm long, about 4 mm wide and slightly channelled; lower half of the leaf is stiff while the upper half becomes quite flowing. Flowering stems about 75 cm long; flower-plumes fairly dense and congested.

DISTRIBUTION: Occurs around a small area of the southern North Island coast from Palliser Bay to the southern Wairarapa, where it grows on coastal cliffs and bluffs, and also a short distance inland. It also occurs on the hills above Okiwi Bay in the Marlborough Sounds.

Chionochloa bromoides

An attractive species which is still uncommon in cultivation. Its bright green colour is distinct and it is useful for associating with golden-leaved plants, especially those with broad leaves. It will tolerate some dryness but is better when grown in soil that does not dry out too much. Being a coastal species it is ideal for growing in coastal gardens. Of all the *Chionochloa* species, this one would probably be the most frost tender. It will not tolerate more than light to medium frosts and is likely to be killed by severe frosts.

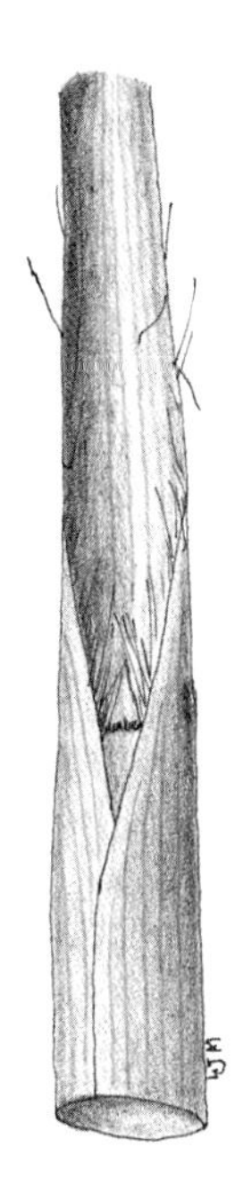

Chionochloa juncea, detail of leaf-sheath and ligule.

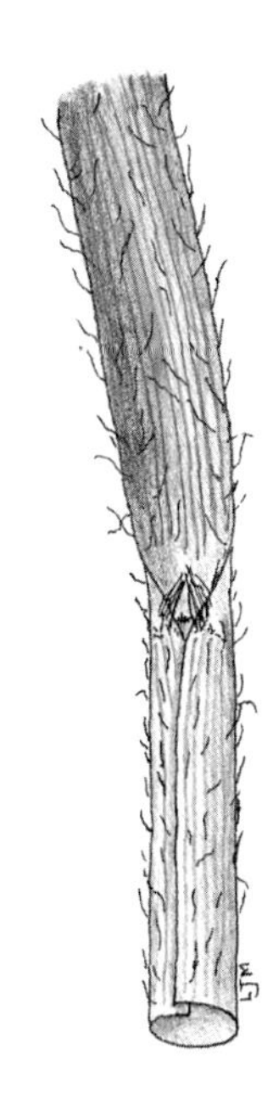

Chionochloa pallens ssp. *pilosa*, detail of leaf-sheath and ligule.

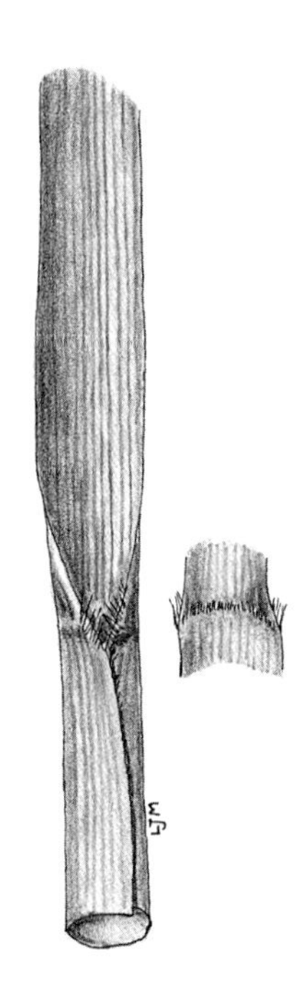

Chionochloa rigida, detail of leaf-sheath and ligule.

DESCRIPTION: A rather stout, bright-green tussock up to 30–40 cm tall, with a flowing or sprawling habit. Flat or shallowly U-shaped leaves up to 50 cm long and 10 mm wide, narrowed to a long, very slender point; leaf-sheaths a shining yellow and up to 15 cm long. Flowering stems up to 70 cm long; the somewhat dense flower-plume about 20 cm long.

DISTRIBUTION: Confined to the north of the North Island, where it occurs northwards from Leigh on the east coast and Maunganui Bluff on the west coast. Also found on some of the offshore islands. Grows on coastal cliffs and bluffs.

Chionochloa conspicua

Hunangamoho, toetoe hunangamoho

This is one of the largest species of *Chionochloa* and deserves to be far more widely used. It is a magnificent grass that rather resembles a toetoe (*Cortaderia*), but from a horticultural viewpoint is far more useful in the garden. It makes a fine feature plant and is bold enough to stand as a solitary specimen or in a shrub border. If there is room to allow several to be planted as a group, it can be very effective and is excellent grown alongside water. It will tolerate quite a variety of conditions, thriving in full sun or quite shady situations, but does not like exposed places where it will receive strong winds or salt-laden sea breezes. It also requires a moist soil but will tolerate dry conditions for limited periods.

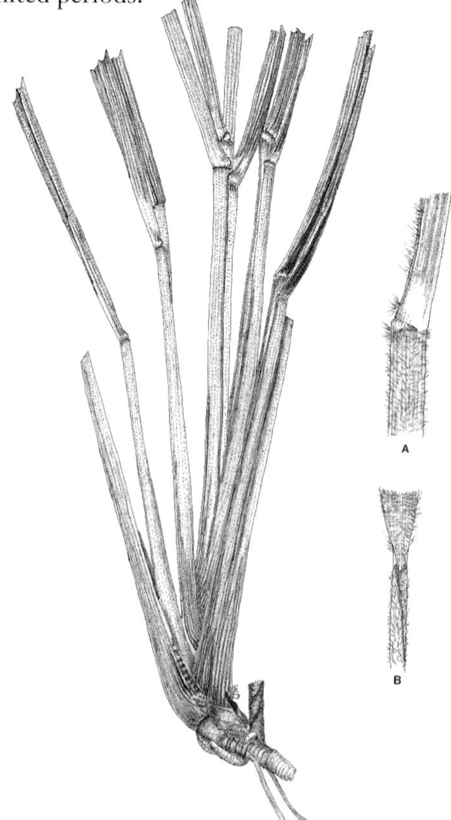

Chionochloa conspicua ssp. *conspicua* showing base of tiller. A and B show details of the ligule at the junction of the leaf-sheath and blade.

DESCRIPTION: Forms dense and robust tussocks up to 1 m or more tall. Leaves up to 1.5 cm wide and up to 1.2 m long, dull, medium green in the upper or inner-facing surface, shining, medium to deep green on the under or outward-facing surface; midrib pale and conspicuous. Open and dainty flower-plumes usually somewhat drooping and up to 45 cm long, carried on stems up to 1.8 m or more tall.

The species consists of two subspecies: *C. conspicua* ssp. *conspicua* and *C. conspicua* ssp. *cunninghamii*. The former is distinguished by the basal leaf-sheaths being rather flattened and silky-hairy, while those of the latter are more rounded and not hairy.

DISTRIBUTION: *C. conspicua* ssp. *conspicua* occurs throughout the higher-rainfall areas of the South Island, although in the lower-rainfall areas east of the Main Divide it is restricted to the Banks and Otago peninsulas. Also occurs on Stewart Island. Grows in forest, scrub, along streamsides and in some cleared areas. Sea level to 1225 m.

C. conspicua ssp. *cunninghamii* occurs in the North Island in limited areas of Northland, Coromandel Peninsula, the East Cape mountains, Mt Pirongia and the Herangi Range, and the Ruahine Range south to Cook Strait. Usually grows in forest, scrub, on cliff faces and in rocky clearings. Sea level to 1500 m.

Chionochloa flavescens

Broad-leaved snow tussock

A large snow grass forming bold tussocks up to 1 m or so tall. As its common name implies, its leaves are relatively broad, compared with other tall tussocks, and in that respect it is fairly distinct.

C. flavescens is not yet very common in cultivation but is well worth growing if it can be obtained. It is very handsome and quite graceful when in flower. Its old leaves break off and form a dense litter around the plant. It requires a moist, well-drained soil and will not stand exposure to salt-laden winds. Best growth is obtained when it is grown in a moist and reasonably fertile soil. In cultivation it flowers during December, but in the wild it is usually about January.

A recently collected form turns a most attractive purplish colour at the onset of winter and holds that colour until about mid-spring. It is most distinct and shows promise of being a great addition to the garden. It is still being trialed and being put through a process of further selection before being released for sale.

DESCRIPTION: A tall, dark green tussock up to 1 m or so tall, which is usually recognised by its broad leaves (up to 1 cm wide) being glaucous green on their upper or inner-facing surfaces and shining, medium green on their under or outer-facing surfaces; leaf may vary from flat to shallowly U-shaped; leaf-sheaths pale to purplish and fracture into short segments. Flowering stems up to 1.5 m tall and the graceful 30 cm flower-plumes are much more open than those of the commonly grown *C. conspicua* and *C. flavicans*.

It comprises four subspecies (ssp. *flavescens*, ssp. *brevis*, ssp. *hirta*, and ssp. *lupeola*), which differ mainly in having hairy or non-hairy leaf-sheaths, or whether there are hairs above the ligule or not. The subspecies most commonly cultivated is ssp. *brevis*, which occurs down the eastern side of the South Island from southern Marlborough to the headwaters of the Waitaki River in South Canterbury.

DISTRIBUTION: Occurs from the Tararua Range in the North Island to the mountains of Nelson, Marlborough, Westland and Canterbury in the South Island, and occurs in grasslands and subalpine scrub from about 750 to 1500 m.

Chionochloa flavicans

A strong-growing tussock up to about 1 m tall, with flowing green foliage. The quite large, compact flower-plumes, rather like a miniature toetoe, make it very easily recognised and unlikely to be confused with any other species. In the nursery trade it is often sold under the incorrect name of 'flavescens', thus creating confusion with the true *C. flavescens*.

This is probably the most widely grown species of *Chionochloa*, and is certainly one of the most useful. In early summer a well-grown plant produces numerous flowering stems on which the flower-plumes are a lovely greenish colour before changing to their typical rich cream as they mature. As the plumes fade they then turn a tawny colour and remain attractive for several months. It can be planted singly or is excellent in groups. It is also most attractive when planted alongside water. The flowering stems last very well when used in floral arrangements and they also dry quite well for use in dried arrangements.

It is a very accommodating plant which will thrive in any well-drained soil in full sun or light shade. While it grows best in a more fertile and reasonably moist soil, it will tolerate a surprising amount of dryness once established.

DESCRIPTION: A stout, rather wide-spreading tussock up to about 1 m tall. Leaves up to 12 mm wide, with the upper or inner-facing surface a dull, light green and the under or outer-facing surface bright green and shining; both surfaces have several distinct veins either side of the midrib, which is quite prominent on the under surface; leaf-sheaths are a pale pinkish purple. Flowering stems can be up to 1.5 m long and the dense flower-plumes are up to 30 cm or more long.

DISTRIBUTION: Confined to the North Island, where it occurs on the Coromandel Peninsula and again from East Cape to southern Hawkes Bay. Grows on cliffs and rock faces from sea level to 975 m. A distinct form (*C. flavicans* forma *temata*) occurs only on Te Mata Peak near Havelock North.

Chionochloa juncea

Chionochloa juncea is a most attractive and quite distinct species which is not yet widely known in cultivation. Its rather stiff leaves spread outwards to give the plant a somewhat fan-shaped appearance. As its name indicates, the leaves have a rush-like appearance. The leaf colour varies from a reddish brown to a purplish brown, and, when the sunlight plays on them the whole plant has a very warm look about it. It is easily grown, requiring only a moist soil in an open situation. Once it becomes more readily available this species should become very popular.

DESCRIPTION: A rigid tussock 60–80 cm tall, with rather rush-like reddish brown foliage. Leaves up to 70 cm long and about 2 mm in diameter; dark brown leaf-sheaths up to 15 cm long and the old leaves remain attached before ultimately falling

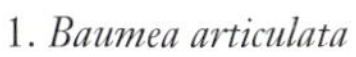

1. *Baumea articulata*

2. A small plant of *Baumea complanata*. The foliage alone makes it an attractive plant.

3. A well-flowered plant of wind grass or gossamer grass (*Anemanthele lessoniana*).

4. *Baumea rubiginosa*

5. The almost white foliage of *Carex albula* and the non-curly leaf tips readily distinguish this species from *C. comans* 'Frosted Curls', which is often wrongly named *C. albula*.

6. *Carex buchananii*

7. *Carex chathamica* is an interesting species from the Chatham Islands.

8. *Carex cirrhosa* is readily distinguished by its small size and distinctively curled leaf-tips.

9. A form of Carex *comans* which has warm-coloured foliage. It is sometimes sold under the name of *C. comans* 'Bronze Form'.

10. *Carex comans* 'Frosted Curls' looks particularly good, either as a single plant or as shown here as a group.

11. *Carex devia*. The flowering spikes of this species stand well above the foliage on very long stems. It naturally occurs in serpentine areas of Nelson.

12. *Carex dissita*. One of the distinguishing characters of this species is the very dark flower and seed spikes, which are almost black when mature.

13. A attractively coloured form of *Carex flagellifera*.

14. *Carex flagellifera* 'Bronze Delight'

15. *Carex gaudichaudiana*. Were it not for the double-folded leaves, this species could easily be mistaken for a grass.

16. Grasses are very effective in containers. *Carex* 'Goldilocks' and *Festuca coxii* in a terracotta pot.

17. *Carex geminata* is mainly used in environmental plantings.

18. Carex *inopinata*

19. *Carex trifida* or tataki grass

20. *Carex testacea* is particularly effective when lit by the winter sun.

21. *Carex secta*: a very handsome and useful species for planting alongside water.

22. *Carex comans* makes an effective edging along the front of a shrub border.

23. The bold and very handsome flower-spikes of *Carex trifida* contrast against the blue-green of its foliage.

24. *Carex ventosa* is a Chatham Islands species which is similar to *C. trifida* but is generally a little smaller.

25. *Carex flagellifera* with *Libertia peregrinans* and *Blechnum pennamarina*, Sonoda Garden, Christchurch.

26. *Carex virgata*

27. *Chionochloa beddiei*. One of the most attractive of the smaller species of *Chionochloa*.

28. An exceptionally well-grown plant of the South Island form of hunangamoho (*Chionochloa conspicua* subspecies *conspicua*).

29. *Chionochloa flavescens* the broad-leaved snow grass.

30. *Chionochloa flavicans* is very suitable for massed plantings.

Above: 31. *Chionochloa pallens*

Top right: 32. *Chionochloa juncea*, as yet little known in gardens, deserves to be more widely known.

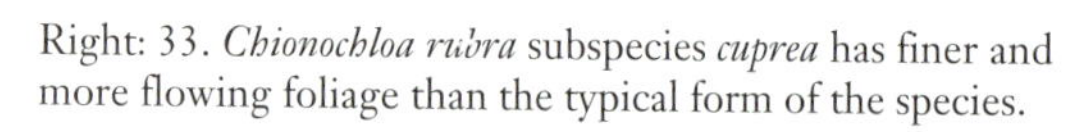

Right: 33. *Chionochloa rubra* subspecies *cuprea* has finer and more flowing foliage than the typical form of the species.

34. *Cortaderia toetoe*

35. *Cortaderia splendens.* This large species can be very imposing where space permits its use.

36. *Desmoshoenus spiralis* or pingao

37. *Elymus solandri* is one of the most attractive of the blue-grey grasses.

38. *Festuca matthewsii*

39. *Festuca coxii*

40. *Festuca novae-zelandiae* or hard tussock

41. *Gahnia procera*

42. *Isolepis nodosus*

43. *Gahnia rigida* is readily distinguished by its stiff erect flowering stems.

44. *Juncus caespiticius*, a small species of rush mostly used for environmental plantings.

45. *Juncus maritimus* var. *australis*

46. *Juncus pallidus* is a bold species with a vertical accent.

47. *Lepidosperma australe*

48. *Leptocarpus similis*, oioi or jointed rush

49. *Luzula ulophylla*

50. A simple arrangement of *Carex flagellifera* with bamboo.

51. *Machaerina sinclairii* (pepepe) has lovely reddish brown flowering plumes.

52. Grasses add interest to the street front planting of a residential garden. Species include *Chionochloa flavicans*, *Carex flagellifera* and *C. comans*, Richmond, Nelson.

53. *Poa cita* or silver tussock.

54. *Poa astonii* is a fine blue-grey grass which rivals *Festuca coxii*.

55. *Schoenoplectus validus* or kuta growing in a swamp.

56. *Schoenus apogon*

57. *Sporodanthus traversii* is a handsome Restiad from the Chatham Islands.

58. *Typha orientalis*, raupo or bulrush

59. Raupo (*Typha orientalis*) is very effective when used in this Japanese garden.

60. *Uncinia egmontiana*

61. A reddish form of *Uncinia uncinata*, the hook grass.

62. Toetoe, *Cortaderia richardii*, used in an environmental planting.

63. Carexes in association with other plants: *Phormium*, *Skimmia*, *Griselinia* and *Melicope*.

below the sheath. Flowering stems up to 90 cm long; the rather sparse flower-plume is up to 20 cm long.

DISTRIBUTION: Restricted to a small area of North Buller in the South Island, where it mainly occurs on the Denniston Plateau and one or two adjoining areas. Occurs in scrub, tussock lands and swampy places, 450–950 m.

Chionochloa pallens

Midribbed snow tussock

This is a handsome snow tussock which is not yet common in cultivation. It usually grows to about 1 m tall, and the foliage often has a pale or slightly yellowish appearance. The flowering stems and plumes are an attractive straw colour and when contrasted against the light green foliage give the whole plant a pleasing appearance. It should be grown in a well-drained, moisture-retentive soil in an open situation.

DESCRIPTION: A stout and rather tall tussock to about 1 m high, usually of a rather pallid appearance. Leaf variable and may be flattish, U-shaped, or the margins somewhat rolled inwards, 8–10 mm wide by 50 cm–1 m long; upper or inward-facing surface a pale greyish green and the lower or outward-facing surface light green and shining; old leaf-sheaths do not fracture but remain intact, and the old leaves usually remain attached. Flowering stems to 1 m or more long; flower- plume rather small and very open.

DISTRIBUTION: Occurs in mountain areas of the North Island from the Raukumara Range southwards. South Island, in the mountains of northern Marlborough and Nelson. Usually in grasslands of low alpine areas, 1100–1700 m.

There are two subspecies, one of which (ssp. *pilosa*) occurs in the northern half of the South Island and the other (ssp. *cadens*) in the southern half.

Chionochloa rigida

Narrow-leaved snow tussock

This is another species which is not yet commonly cultivated but could be more widely used. It is very hardy and, once established, is tolerant of fairly dry conditions. In addition, its flowing habit and particularly its colour are very useful for contrasting with other plants or grasses.

DESCRIPTION: A tall and stout tussock up to 1 m tall, usually a tawny-green or golden colour. Leaves up to about 80 cm long and 7 mm wide, flat, shallowly U-shaped or with the margins rolled slightly inwards; upper or inner-facing surfaces a dull greyish green and the under or outer-facing surfaces a light to yellowish green and shining; the dry tips of the leaves help to give this tussock its tawny or golden colour; leaf-sheaths up to 30 cm long, dark brown towards the base, fracturing into segments with age, the old leaves break off with part of the sheath and form a dense litter around the plant. Flowering stems up to 1.5 m long; loose and open flower-plume about 30 cm long.

DISTRIBUTION: Confined to the South Island, occurring south from Banks Peninsula and the Rakaia River east of the Main Divide, and Lake Kaniere on the west.

Two subspecies (ssp. *rigida* and ssp. *amara*) are recognised. The former occurs only east of the Main Divide and as well as being more common, it is also the one usually cultivated. It grows from lowland to low alpine areas (up to 1700 m) and is one of the two or three species that high-country run-holders and musterers refer to as snow grass.

Chionochloa rubra

Red tussock

This is probably the third most commonly cultivated species. It is a very handsome plant and certainly deserves to be far more widely used in horticulture, particularly as it is very hardy and has the added advantage that it is more amenable in cultivation than some others. Usually it is grown purely for its foliage and form, although a well-flowered plant does have a certain attraction.

C. rubra is divided into three subspecies, and the one usually grown is *C. rubra* ssp. *cuprea*, which occurs down the eastern side of the South Island from North Canterbury to Fiordland and also on Stewart Island.

Of that subspecies, there is no doubt that the Southland and southern Otago forms are the best to grow in gardens, and of those, it is considered that the one which grows on the Southland Plains, particularly around Invercargill, is the finest. When well grown it forms large, flowing tussocks which can be up to 1.6 m tall and about 1.8 m across. Its foliage is finer and more flowing than that of the other forms and, when rippled by the wind, provides some lovely flowing effects. Throughout the growing season this tussock is the typical tawny colour associated with the tall tussock grasslands, but with the advent of cooler autumn and winter conditions it takes on the very attractive reddish and orange tones for which the species is named.

The red tussock is a most adaptable plant which will grow in exposed, windy situations, in low-fertility soils, and will tolerate relatively wet or dry soil conditions. It is bold enough to use as an individual specimen plant but, if space permits, there is no doubt that several should be planted as a group. It is also a very useful plant for helping to provide a wildlife habitat, particularly when used as a marginal plant around wetland areas.

DESCRIPTION: A tall, robust tussock 1–1.6 m tall, with gracefully flowing foliage.The colour of the tussocks varies from a greenish tawny colour to reddish or even a coppery colour. The very slender leaves are 1–1.7 m long and 2–3 mm wide; this slenderness is caused by the margins being heavily rolled inwards so that the leaves appear to be almost round; when run through the hand the leaves are slightly rough to the touch; the leaf-sheaths up to 30 cm long, dark brown and when old either remain whole or fracture into short segments; margins separate and coil. Flowering stems up to 1.5 m long; rather sparse and open flower-plumes up to 45 cm long. Generally the flower-plumes remain partly within or just above the foliage.

DISTRIBUTION: Throughout the North, South and Stewart Islands from the Volcanic Plateau southwards. In the far south it attains its greatest development in parts of Otago and Southland.

It is divided into three subspecies and one variety. *C. rubra* ssp. *rubra* occurs in the mountains of the North Island, Marlborough and southwards to North Canterbury; *C. rubra* ssp. *rubra* var. *inermis* is confined to Mt Egmont; ssp. *cuprea* grows from North Canterbury to Fiordland and Stewart Island; and ssp. *occulta* occurs in Nelson and Westland as far south as the Cascade Plateau. Lowland to low alpine. Sea level to 1500 m.

CORTADERIA
Gramineae

From *cortadera*, the Argentinean name for the pampas grass.

This genus contains the well-known toetoe, the largest of our native grasses. These plants form large and dense clumps or tussocks 1.5–2.5 m tall, and their leaves have roughened margins which are very sharp and can inflict painful cuts on the unwary. The flowering stems rise to about 3–6 m tall and bear very handsome and showy flower-plumes, usually of a buff to yellowish colour. The genus contains about 25 species of which five are endemic to New Zealand, one to Papua-New Guinea and the remainder to South America.

Two of the South American species are grown in New Zealand and have become naturalised. One (*C. jubata*), the purple pampas grass, is regarded as being a serious pest. The native species are generally known as toetoe, which is frequently mispronounced and misspelt as 'toitoi'. Similarly, many New Zealanders do not know the difference between the native toetoe and the introduced pampas grass and generally refer to the latter as toetoe. Alternative common names for the native species are kakaho, toetoe kakaho and cutty grass.

The native species of *Cortaderia* are easily distinguished from the introduced pampas grasses by having a white, waxy bloom on their leaf-sheaths and conspicuous

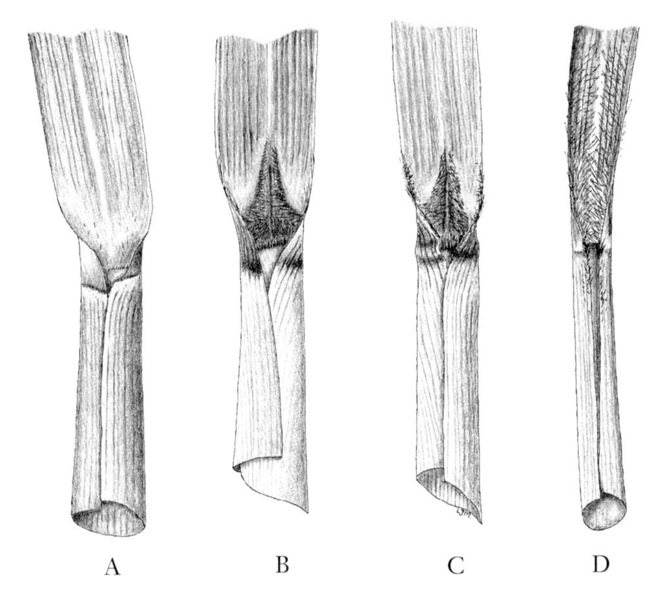

Details of the ligules and leaf-sheaths of (A): *Cortaderia fulvida;* (B): *C. richardii;* (C): *C. toetoe;* (D): *C. turbaria*. In particular, note the relative lengths of the hairs forming the fringe around the inside of the ligules.

nerves or veins between their midribs and the leaf margins. The old, dead leaf-sheaths of the native species do not curl into a spiral as do the old leaf-sheaths of the pampas grasses. Generally, the native species are earlier flowering, although that is by no means universal.

The species are easily cultivated and grow well in a variety of soils from heavy to sandy, and swampy to dry situations. They also grow from the coast to low mountain areas and are very wind tolerant. Where space permits they make fine landscape plants and, when planted along a fenceline or similar situation, provide very good low shelter. About the only maintenance that they require is the removal of the old flowering stems in the late autumn and a grooming to get rid of some of the dead foliage. Long-handled lopping shears and a pair of gloves make this operation much easier. Propagation is usually by seed, although selected plants can be propagated by division. Younger plants are more easily divided, and the divisions grow more readily than those from mature plants.

Cortaderia fulvida

Toetoe

While still quite a large plant, it is usually relatively smaller than the other species and is perhaps more useful for growing where space is rather limited. It usually flowers between late October and early December.

DESCRIPTION: Forms large tussocks 1.5–2.5 m tall at flowering. Leaves 1–2 m long and 1.5–4 cm wide, bluish green, dull on the upper surface and shining beneath. Flower-stems gracefully drooping and usually golden but may be pinkish when they first emerge. It can be distinguished from the other species mainly by having a row of short hairs, about 1 mm long, on the ligule (where the leaf-blade joins the sheath) and by the absence of hairs above the ligule. Apart from *C. splendens*, it has the widest leaves of any other native species.

DISTRIBUTION: Occurs throughout the North Island, where it is common on stream banks, swamp edges and in hilly terrain. Recently collected material from near Pakawau, Golden Bay, in the South Island appears to be this species, as does material collected from Mt Burnett nearer to Collingwood. Sea level to about 1100 m.

Cortaderia richardii

Toetoe

It is also a most versatile species and is suitable for growing in a wide variety of soils and situations. Flowering usually occurs from December to January.

DESCRIPTION: In general appearance this species is similar to *C. fulvida* and *C. toetoe* but differs from *C. fulvida* in being up to 3 m or so tall at flowering, and in its leaves being only 1–2 cm wide. Another distinguishing character is that the ligule has a row of 1–3 mm-long hairs, and often there are some very fine hairs above it. Leaves up to 2 m long, dull, medium green above and shining beneath. Flower-plumes 30–60 cm long and, as with *C. fulvida*, droop gracefully, however they are a little stiffer and do not have the fullness of that species.

DISTRIBUTION: Confined to the South and Stewart Islands, where it grows on open stream banks, in scrublands, wet places, hillsides and sand dunes. Sea level to 600 m.

Cortaderia splendens

Toetoe

This is a coastal species and is noted for having stout rhizomes which may extend through sand for a number of metres to establish a new plant. My only experience with growing this species was in a relatively heavy soil and there was no evidence it was going to produce any rhizomes. Perhaps this character only becomes evident in light sandy soils. Flowering is usually in early December.

DESCRIPTION: A large and vigorous plant which may be up to 6 m tall at flowering. Leaves up to 3 m long and 3–5 cm wide; margins are not as harsh as those of the other species. Apart from its large size and very wide leaves, it has a row of 2–5 mm-long hairs on the ligule and it is also densely, long hairy above the ligule with the hairs mainly confined to the midrib and leaf margin. Flowering plumes about 75 cm long, light golden yellow and erect or drooping.

DISTRIBUTION: Confined to the upper part of the North Island from Kawhia northwards. Also occurs on the Three Kings and the east coast offshore islands to the Coromandel Peninsula. Grows on sand dunes, rocks and coastal cliff faces.

Cortaderia toetoe

Toetoe

This is one of the most commonly grown species and can be used for similar purposes to the other species. Where space permits it is worth planting several in a group. Flowering usually occurs in January.

DESCRIPTION: Forms dense tussocks and is up to 4 m tall at flowering. Leaves are up to 2 m long and 1.5–3 cm wide, dull, slightly greyish green above and shining beneath, margins very harsh and scabrid. One of its main distinguishing characters is the line of 2–5 mm-long hairs on the ligule, above which the leaf-blade is densely covered with long hairs. Flowering plume 60–100 cm long and often rather rigid and erect.

DISTRIBUTION: Confined to the North Island from about Tauranga to Wellington. Occurs in swamps, bush clearings, along roadsides, on sand-dunes and in coastal areas.

Cortaderia turbaria

Toetoe

This is a fairly recently discovered species from the Chatham Islands. I have not grown it long enough to be able to adequately compare it with the other species.

DESCRIPTION: Grows to about 2 m tall, with leaves only about 1 cm wide. One of its main distinguishing characters is the base of the leaf, which is densely hairy above the ligule. Flowering plume up to 30 cm long.

DISTRIBUTION: Chatham Islands.

CYPERUS
Cyperaceae

From the old Greek name (*kypeiros*) for a sedge. Also known as umbrella sedge.

Cyperus is a large genus of mainly tropical and subtropical species, although there are some which grow in more temperate climates. They are known as umbrella sedges because their inflorescences sit atop a cluster of leafy bracts, which gives them an umbrella-like appearance. They are mainly moisture-loving plants with some actually preferring to grow in water.

Out of over 600 species, only one is native to New Zealand, although some 13 introduced species have become naturalised. Propagation is by seed or division. Some species can be propagated by stem cuttings of the flower-head which can be rooted in a peat and sand mixture in close conditions. It is possible that the native species could also be propagated in this manner.

Cyperus ustulatus
Giant umbrella sedge, toetoe upokotangata

Generally, *C. ustulatus* is considered too large and coarse for use in all but the largest of areas, but it does have a certain character and could be useful for planting in wet areas or alongside water. If required, it can actually be grown in shallow water. Being a mainly coastal plant, it could be used in revegetation or environmental plantings in coastal areas, particularly where there is damp or wet ground. It is easily grown in a variety of soils and situations, as long as conditions are not too dry. At one time Maori used the foliage for thatching.

DESCRIPTION: A large and robust clump- or tussock-forming plant 60–100 cm tall. Leaves 60–120 cm long by 1–1.5 cm wide, quite tough, medium to deep green, prominently keeled beneath and with minute but sharp teeth along the margins and the keel. Flowering stems up to 1.2 m or more, distinctly three-angled; at the top of the flower stem is a cluster of long, leafy bracts atop which are clustered the dark brown, shining spikelets.

DISTRIBUTION: Kermadec Islands, throughout the North Island, and in the South Island as far south as Motukarara and the Rakaia River mouth on the east, and Fiordland on the west; also on the Chatham Islands. Occurs in lowland areas, mainly in damp ground near rivers and especially near the coast.

DESMOSCHOENUS
Cyperaceae

A genus of but one species which is confined to New Zealand. It is related to *Scirpus*, from which it is distinguished by its leaves being harshly scabrid along their margins and by the inflorescence being a contracted panicle.

Desmoschoenus spiralis
Pingao

From the Greek *desmos*, a bond, and *schoenus*, perhaps referring to its affinity with *schoenus*. This species is easily recognised by its overall yellow-green or warm golden colour and its stiffly, arching leaves, which feel harsh when run through the fingers and are arranged spirally around the stem. Its dark reddish brown, densely congested flower-spikes are another distinguishing feature. It is quite ornamental and is one of those plants which can be described as having an architectural character. It is easily grown if given a light, well-drained (preferably sandy) soil in full sun. An open situation is essential if the foliage is to develop its lovely golden or yellowish colour. Propagation is usually by seed, but plants can also be divided. Young plants provide the most satisfactory divisions.

In nature pingao is confined to coastal sand-dunes, and before the introduction of marram grass it was one of the principal sand binders, helping to fix the dunes and prevent their erosion. Destruction of its habitat, as well as the depredations of browsing animals such as hares, rabbits and farm stock, have greatly reduced its former abundance. In the past it was a valuable plant to Maori, who used it for weaving. In some areas environmental groups are now active in re-planting sand dunes with pingao.

DESCRIPTION: A stout and rather rigid plant 60–90 cm tall, with thick underground rhizomes. Tufted leaves stiff and hard to the touch, yellow-green to golden; upper or inward-facing surface is channelled and the under or outward-facing surface is keeled. Flower-stem up to 90 cm tall; dark reddish brown flower-head 7–20 cm long.

DISTRIBUTION: Found in the North, South, Stewart and Chatham Islands, on coastal sand-dunes.

ELEOCHARIS
Cyperaceae

From the Greek *helodes*, marshy, and *charis*, grace or loveliness.

Grass-like or rush-like plants which actually belong to the sedge family. They are annual or perennial, leafless, grass-like or rush-like herbs. What appear to be their leaves are, in fact, flowering stems which perform the functions of true leaves. Their flowering parts are single spikelets borne at the tips of the stems. It is a cosmopolitan genus of about 200 species. Five species occur in New Zealand, one of which is restricted to New Zealand, with the rest also occurring in Australia.

Eleocharis is mainly useful for growing in boggy areas, around the margins of ponds, or even in shallow water. The easiest method of propagation is by division.

Eleocharis acuta
Spike rush

While it is not highly ornamental, this species is useful for growing in damp or boggy soil. Its bright green stems have a fresh appearance and it would be useful for associating with yellow or yellow-variegated plants. It will also grow in shallow water close to the edges of ponds, where it can provide shelter for fish, frogs and other pond wildlife.

DESCRIPTION: A slowly spreading plant up to 50 cm tall or, occasionally, to 90 cm.

Stems stiffly erect, 1–2 mm in diameter, bright green or a pale golden brown. Spikelets 5–25 x 2–5 mm, cylindrical and pointed at their tips.

DISTRIBUTION: Kermadec, North, South, Stewart and Chatham Islands. Occurs in damp, swampy ground and along stream and lake margins. Sea level to 1100 m.

Eleocharis sphacelata

Ngawha, great spike rush, kuta, kutakuta

A distinct and strongly growing species which is distinguished by its thick, cylindrical, hollow stems, which are internally divided by partitions and have quite a sponge-like feel to them. It grows from 60 cm to 1 m tall and may be further identified by the internal partitions giving the outside of the stem an apparently jointed appearance. It produces large club-like flower-spikes at the tips of the stems.

When growing well, *E. sphacelata* is quite ornamental and is an attractive plant for growing in the shallow water near the margin of a pond, where its creeping roots will slowly spread outwards. It can be grown in quite small ponds and could even be grown in a large tub. If it becomes too large, it is easily reduced in size. The stems were and still are used by Maori for weaving soft mats and baskets.

DESCRIPTION: A strong-growing plant with a thick, creeping rhizome 1–1.5 cm in diameter. Stems 30–90 cm tall and 4–12 mm in diameter; internally divided by transverse partitions at 1–10 cm intervals; partitions visible through the outer wall of the stem to give them a jointed appearance. Basal sheaths grey and papery. Flowering spike 2.5–5 cm long, 0.5–1 cm in diameter, light brown to reddish brown.

DISTRIBUTION: North Island, distributed throughout, but not so common south of Waitara and Wairoa. South Island, in Nelson, Marlborough, Westland, and Southland near Invercargill; very rare in Canterbury. Stewart Island. Occurs in very wet places, in swamps and around lake edges. Lower parts usually submerged in water. Sea level to 800 m.

ELYMUS

Gramineae

From the Greek *elymos*, the classical name for millet.

The species are either tufted or rhizomatous perennial grasses with flat or, rarely, rolled leaves. Their inflorescences are stout to slender, and are distinguished by long, bristle-like awns. Some of the species are valued for their attractive blue-green foliage. Of the 150 species world-wide, only about four are native to New Zealand, and of those, only one is really worth cultivating.

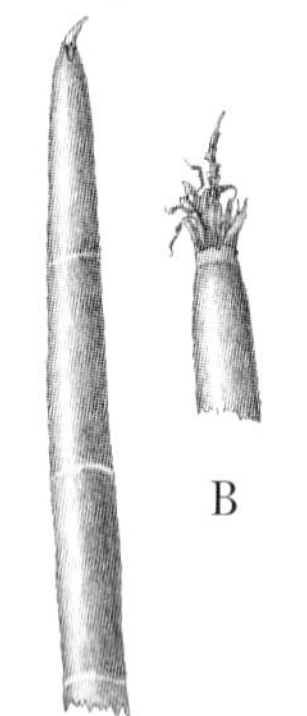

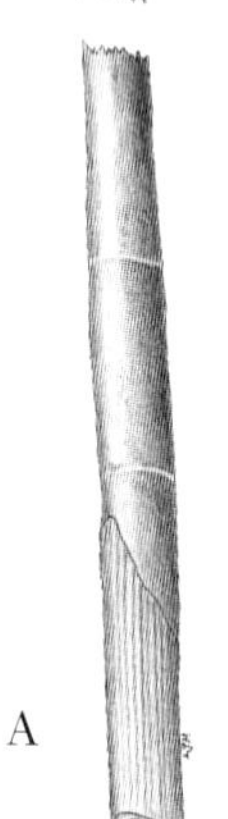

Eleocharis sphacelata showing details of (A): the stem and the sheath at its base; (B): an old inflorescence at the tip.

Elymus solandri

Blue grass, blue wheat grass

This variable species is easily recognised because of its grey-green to beautifully blue-grey foliage. It forms spreading tufts up to 30 cm tall and 50 cm across. Its flower-spikes are also quite distinctive because they have long awns or bristles projecting from where each seed is.

The usually cultivated form has to be one of the bluest of all grasses and certainly one of the most desirable of our native species to grow in the garden. Compared with other forms of *E. solandri*, it has quite broad leaves and forms rather bold clumps. Initally the foliage lies almost flat on the ground, but as the plant becomes larger it builds up to form a low mound about 20 cm high by about 50 cm across. It is an excellent plant for the front of a border and is sufficiently outstanding to grow as a single specimen, or a great effect is obtained if several are planted as a group.

E. solandri should be grown in an open situation and is quite tolerant of a variety of soils, providing they are well-drained. Once established it will tolerate prolonged periods of dry conditions. Seed is by far the easiest means of propagation, but it can be divided should the necessity arise.

On other forms of this species the leaves can be narrow and the plant stands up more rather than tending to lie on the ground. Usually they are more greyish or grey-green and do not have the outstanding colour of the form described.

DESCRIPTION: A laxly tufted plant 40–50 cm across and up to 20 cm or more high. Leaves 5–28 cm long and 2–7 mm wide, flat or strongly in-rolled, strongly glaucous or grey-green. Flowering stems 40–100 cm long, smooth and slender, often lying almost flat on the ground; flower panicle spike-like with long, prominent awns.

DISTRIBUTION: North and South Islands. Occurs throughout, usually on rocky sites such as cliffs, riverbeds, loose rocky debris and tussock grassland. It is palatable and often occurs only in places inaccessible to browsing animals. Sea level to 1500 m.

FESTUCA

Gramineae

From the latin *festuca*, stalk or stem; in Pliny the wild oat growing among the barley.

A genus of perennial grasses, tufted or spreading by underground stems (New Zealand species are mostly tufted). Their leaves may be flat, folded or with the margins rolled inwards. In many respects they resemble *Poa* but differ in the glumes (the chaffy scales of the seed-head) being rounded on their backs rather than keeled as in *Poa*. The genus contains some 300 species, mainly in the temperate and colder regions of both hemispheres. There are about six species native to New Zealand. Propagation is most easily carried out by division, but they are also easily raised from seed.

Festuca "Banks Peninsula"

Blue tussock

This is an as yet unnamed species which occurs on Banks Peninsula, hence the reason for its tag-name. It has fine, blue-green foliage. Its growth habit and stiff flowering stems make it distinct from other blue-green tussocks. It will tolerate quite dry conditions and is useful for planting in dry soils. The best foliage colour is maintained if plants are divided about every three years.

DESCRIPTION: A smaller tussock 30–50 cm tall, of a somewhat stiff habit with the outer leaves spreading. Leaves 30–40 cm long, about 0.5 mm in diameter, heavily rolled and blue-green in colour. Flowering stems to 70 cm long and standing stiffly above the plant.

DISTRIBUTION: Apparently confined to Banks Peninsula.

Festuca coxii

This is a particularly lovely blue-green tussock which deserves to be far more widely grown. In suitable conditions the foliage becomes a really good bluish colour. While it will tolerate a considerable amount of drought, it does far better in soil that does not dry out too much, and will succeed in sun or indirect shade. It is useful for edging or as foreground groups. Try a group planting with the plants more widely spaced and grow a silver-foliaged carpeting plant in between. Plants should be divided every three years or so to maintain the best foliage colour.

A certain amount of confusion exists in nurseries and garden centres concerning this plant. A form of the introduced *F. glauca* is sometimes mistakenly grown as *F. coxii*, with the result that some have come to believe that it is our native species. The two are quite distinct, the introduced plant having shorter and stiffer leaves which are an intense grey-blue.

DESCRIPTION: A small tussock of flowing habit, up to 35 cm tall. Leaves to about 40 cm long and about 1 mm wide, blue- or greyish green, pointed tips whitened; leaf margins so tightly inrolled that the leaf appears to be cylindrical. Flowering stems 40–45 cm long, flowering panicles up to 4 cm long.

DISTRIBUTION: Confined to the Chatham Islands, where it grows on rocks and sands near the seashore.

Festuca matthewsii

This is a medium-sized, grey-green or glaucous tussock, 25–50 cm tall. It has a rather stiffly erect habit of growth, and the flowering stems greatly over-top the foliage. This is a little-known species which could be more widely used. Its stiff habit contrasts with the flowing lines of species such as *F. coxii*, while its grey-green colour is more subtle than the stronger blue-green of *F. coxii*. Although it grows best in a soil that does not become too dry, it is also well-adapted for growing in dry soils.

DESCRIPTION: Densely tufted, 20–50 cm tall, rather erect habit of growth and usually a grey-green or dull glaucous colour. Leaves 30–50 cm long, strongly inrolled, 0.75–1 mm in diameter, smooth or slightly harsh to the touch. Flowering stems much longer than the leaves, few-flowered, with a loose head of flattened spikelets.

DISTRIBUTION: South Island, where it occurs in subalpine grasslands throughout; usually in snow tussock-herbfields and grasslands in valley bottoms of the wetter regions. In the drier eastern areas where the snow tussocks have been depleted by burning it is quite common and forms distinct tussocks. 700–1500 m.

Festuca multinodus

As well as being a distinct and easily recognised species, this is also one which should be more widely known. The rather spikey leaves are greyish green and they contrast most attractively with the reddish purple of the young stems. With its sprawling or trailing habit, it is ideal for growing in a container, the front of a border or along an edge where it can trail over. It is best grown in a soil that does not dry out too much. It can survive in full sun as long as it does not become too dry; otherwise plant in indirect shade where it will receive some light. It is easily propagated by division or from self-rooted pieces which occur where the stems come in contact with moist soil.

DESCRIPTION: A densely tufted grass with sprawling or trailing stems which become more upright towards their tips. Stems purplish towards their tips, 15–40 cm long, branching, leaves quite widely spaced along them. Leaves 8.5–12 cm long, 0.8–1 mm in diameter, tightly rolled and almost cylindrical; sheaths 2.5–5 cm long and split to the base down one side. Flowering stems extending beyond the leaves; flowering panicle 3–6 cm long.

DISTRIBUTION: Occurs in the southern North Island, where it is found around the Wellington coastline, and in the South island in the Awatere Valley, on Banks Peninsula and in Central Otago. Grows on coastal cliffs and bluffs, and in snow-tussock grasslands and herbfields. Sea level to 1400 m.

Festuca novae-zelandiae

Fescue tussock, hard tussock

This is a common component of low-tussock grassland, particularly in the higher country, and as a consequence, its merits as a garden plant are often overlooked. It is a rather variable species with some forms being much better than others. Its leaves are rigid and erect, so much so in some forms that the whole plant is very dense and erect. On other forms the leaves are still stiff but rather more spreading, giving the plant a more pleasing form. The new leaves are green and are intermingled with the old, dead ones, which is what gives this species its characteristic appearance. It is a hardy tussock which will tolerate considerable drought and exposure, and is very useful for growing in difficult situations. Although it makes better growth in more favourable conditions, it should not be too well treated or it will lose its essential character. It is easily propagated from seed, and selected forms should be increased by division.

DESCRIPTION: An erect, densely tufted, tawny tussock, 60–70 cm tall. Leaves 15–60 cm long x 0.5–1 mm in diameter, green to slightly greyish, rough to the touch, tips sharply pointed; margins very tightly inrolled to make the leaf appear cylindrical. Flowering stems to 30–70 cm tall; flowering panicle 5–12 cm long, rather open.

DISTRIBUTION: North and South Islands in dry grasslands throughout, from the

Kaimanawa and Ruahine Ranges southwards. Usually in montane to lower subalpine regions. 300–1200 m.

GAHNIA
Cyperaceae

A commemorative name in honour of the German botanist Gahn.

A genus of large sedges, often forming very large tussocks and usually with conspicuous flowering stems. Their seeds are in the form of nuts, which hang from the inflorescence by long filaments. The colours of the nuts of the various species vary from orange to orange-brown, to reddish or very dark blackish brown.

Generally they are not difficult to cultivate but resent disturbance of their roots and, once planted, should not be disturbed. The best means of propagation is by seed, which should be dry-stored for about two months before sowing. Germination can take up to 10 months or longer. As soon as the seedlings are large enough to handle they should be transplanted into individual containers. Established plants are hardy enough, but young plants may be damaged or killed by severe frosts. Few nurseries offer gahnias for sale.

The genus extends from New Zealand and Australia to the Pacific islands, Malaysia, China and Japan. Of the six native species, one extends to some of the Pacific islands and the remaining five are confined to New Zealand. Generally they are known as giant sedges or cutty grasses, and only three species appear to have Maori common names.

Gahnia lacera
Tarangarara

This species is distinguished by the fact that it does not form a dense tussock but slowly spreads outwards by means of woody underground stems or rhizomes. It is quite an attractive species and appears to be more easily grown than some of the others. It is best grown in shade, in a moist but well-drained soil. Being a forest dweller, it is ideal for planting under trees.

DESCRIPTION: A thickly tufted, yellowish green plant, 60 cm–1.5 m tall, with leafy stems. Leaves equal to or longer than the stems, up to 9 mm wide, flat or shallowly U-shaped; margins sharp with minute teeth. Flowering panicle rigid, 20–40 cm long and rather dense. Nut 3.5–4.5 x about 2 mm, black and shining.

DISTRIBUTION: Confined to the North Island, where it occurs from North Cape southwards to about Wanganui. Uncommon south of the Waikato.

Gahnia procera

Gahnia procera is one of the smaller species, and with its deep green, shining foliage and gracefully drooping flowering panicles, is quite a handsome plant. It is not too difficult to grow and will tolerate a fairly wet soil but is better planted in a moist, well-drained soil. It is mainly a forest plant and prefers to be grown in a shady situation.

DESCRIPTION: Forms stout and robust tufts or tussocks, 45–90 cm tall. Leaves 60 cm–1 m long, about 1 cm wide, and narrowed to long, slender points, upper surface deep green. Flowering stems up to 1 m or more long; flowering panicle 45–70 cm long, dark coloured, drooping. Nuts 5–6.5 x 2–2.5 mm, brownish orange.

DISTRIBUTION: In the North Island occurs in mountain forests southwards from about Thames, and in the South Island in Nelson, Westland, Fiordland and one locality in Canterbury; also on Stewart Island. Usually in forest, bog or scrub. Descends to sea level in the far south.

Gahnia setifolia

Mapere

Gahnia setifolia is one of the larger species and too large for small gardens. However, where space permits it makes a magnificent specimen. The long, dark-coloured, drooping flower panicles make it a very graceful and striking plant. It should be planted in a moist, well-drained soil and will grow equally well in sun or light shade. Not infrequently, this species can be seen growing in surprisingly dry situations, such as on the edges of road banks, which would seem to indicate that it does not necessarily require a constantly moist soil.

DESCRIPTION: A large tussock-forming species, 1–2.5 m tall. Leaves 1–2 m long, 8–10 mm wide, harsh to the touch because of several longitudinal rows of minute teeth between the leaf margins and the midrib; the margins also have numerous minute teeth which make them very sharp. Flowering stems usually a little longer than the leaves; flower panicles 40–70 cm long, drooping, dark brownish to almost black. Nuts 3.5–4 x about 2mm, reddish brown, smooth and shining.

DISTRIBUTION: Occurs throughout the North Island but not so common in the central part of the island. In the South Island confined to Nelson and Marlborough Sounds. Usually in light forest and scrub. Sea level to 450 m.

Gahnia xanthocarpa

Giant sedge

This is a magnificent plant which is too large for all but the largest of gardens. It forms large tussocks up to 2 m across with dark green foliage, above which the plumed, flowering stems tower to about 4 m. The leaves have sharp cutting edges, which give rise to one of its common names, 'giant cutty grass'.

Where there is room for it to be grown, it can make a most imposing specimen, particularly when it flowers. The flowering plumes are a fawn or light brown and droop gracefully from the erect stems. It is also used for re-vegetation work in environmental plantings.

DESCRIPTION: A very stout plant forming large tussocks up to about 1.5 m tall and 2 m across. Leaves as long as, or slightly shorter than, the flowering stems, 1.5 cm or more wide. Flowering stems stout, about 1 cm in diameter, 3–4 m tall; flower panicles 60–150 cm long, much branched, drooping, light brown.

DISTRIBUTION: North Island, mostly north of about Thames and south of Wanganui. South Island, in Nelson, Marlborough, Westland and rare in Canterbury. In lowland forest or bog. Near sea level to 420 m.

HIEROCHLOE
Gramineae

From the Greek *hieros*, sacred, and *chloa*, grass, in allusion to its use in religious ceremonies.

A small genus of scented grasses. The leaves are flat with quite long sheaths and the flower spikelets are in open or close panicles. These are hardy grasses which grow in damp places and are easily propagated by seed or division. The species are distributed throughout the temperate and colder zones of both hemispheres. There are seven species in New Zealand.

The common name of holy grass refers to their customary use in northern Europe, where it was strewn before church doorways on saints' days. When drying, the leaves emit a fragrance which has variously been likened to vanilla or newly mown hay.

Hierochloe redolens
Scented holy grass, karetu

The leaves, with their glaucous green upper surfaces and shining under surfaces, contrast effectively with the reddish purple leaf-sheaths to make this an attractive plant. It is easily grown in any moist soil that is reasonably well-drained, preferably in shade or semi-shade. If it shows a tendency to spread by its creeping rhizomes, it is easily kept in check. Maori women formerly wove the sweet-scented karetu into waist girdles and necklaces.

DESCRIPTION: A tufted grass growing 45–90 cm tall, often spreading by means of creeping rhizomes. Leaves 14–26 cm long, 8–12 mm wide, dull and slightly glaucous green on the upper or inward-facing surface and bright, shining green on the under or outward-facing surface; sheath long, reddish purple. Flowering stems to 1.3 m tall; flower panicle open and yellowish brown.

DISTRIBUTION: Found throughout the North, South, Stewart, Chatham and Campbell Islands, in wet grasslands and grassland-scrubland, particularly on moist rock-faces and banks. Sea level to 1200 m. Also occurs in Tasmania, Southeast Australia and Tierra del Fuego.

ISOLEPIS
Cyperaceae

From the Greek *isos*, a equal, and *lepis*, a scale, referring to the scale-like glumes.

A genus of grass-like plants of the sedge family, formerly included with *Scirpus*, it has once again been segregated as a genus of its own. Mostly they are tufted although some have creeping rhizomes. Generally they have quite fine leaves and the flowering stems are leaf-like. The flowering spikelets are at the tips of the stems, either singly or several together. There are about 40 species worldwide, and there are about 14 New Zealand native species.

One or two are quite pleasing little plants for moist or boggy soils. They grow best in open conditions and will succeed in light, indirect shade. Propagation is most easily carried out by division.

Isolepis habra

This species forms small and dense mop-like tufts, which are like heads of bright green hair. It is easily grown if planted in a moist soil in light, indirect shade.

DESCRIPTION: A densely tufted, light green plant to about 20 cm high. Leaves and stems thin and grassy, about 0.5 mm in diameter, leaf-sheaths usually reddish purple. Flowering spikelets 2.5–4 x 2–3 mm, 1–3 at the tip of each stem.

DISTRIBUTION: In the North Island from about the southern Waikato southwards, and in the South Island from Nelson to Fiordland and Southland (rare in Marlborough, Canterbury and Otago), and on Stewart, Chatham, Auckland and Campbell Islands. Sea level to 1500 m.

Isolepis nodosa

A rather strong and dense, rush-like plant with a short, creeping rhizome. It is usually 70–90 cm tall, and the stems have small, globular, brown flower-heads at their tips. This species is used for the re-vegetation of wetlands in environmental plantings and for assisting with the treatment of waste water.

DESCRIPTION: Rhizome short and stout, 5–10 mm in diameter. Stems 30–90 cm tall, about 2 mm in diameter, densely crowded, rush-like. Leaves reduced to basal sheaths. Flower-head an apparently solitary, rounded head, 0.7–1.5 mm wide.

DISTRIBUTION: Kermadec, North, South, Stewart and Chatham Islands. Abundant throughout, especially near the coast. Sea level to 600 m.

JUNCUS
Juncaceae

From the Latin *iuncus*, a rush, derived from *iungere*, to join or to bind; it alludes to the ancient use of the stems for tying.

Commonly known as rushes, the leaves of plants in this genus may be flat and grass-like, like a flattened tube, or channelled, cylindrical or stem-like, or reduced to sheaths at the bases of the stems. The small, green or brown flowers may be produced in dense ball-like clusters, in more openly branched clusters or in quite widely branched inflorescences.

Most *Juncus* grow in very moist soils and wet places, such as bogs and along the margins of water areas. Only a few are valued as garden plants, although some others are very useful for environmental plantings, such as in waste-water treatment areas, or for re-vegetation plantings. In the garden their distinct form gives height and foliage contrast, particularly where there is a wet area that is difficult for establishing other plants. They will grow perfectly well in full sun but will also grow reasonably well in partial shade. Some species can be planted in shallow water (about 8–10 cm deep) around pond margins. They can also be planted in containers which are then plunged in the pond. This can make it much easier to manage them. Propagation is easiest by division, although they can be raised from seed if desired.

The Maori common name for a number of similar species is 'wiwi'. There are some 300 species worldwide. Sixteen species are native to New Zealand, and a further 31 introduced species have become naturalised.

Juncus caespiticius

This species is probably of more use in environmental plantings than in the garden, although some may consider that it does have a little horticultural merit. Its low, pale green, grassy tufts are not unattractive, and during the colder months of the year the leaf margins and tips take on a reddish purple hue. It will grow in swampy conditions and is adapted for growing where the water is brackish.

DESCRIPTION: Small, pale green, grass-like tufts, 15–20 cm tall. Leaves 15–20 cm long, 4–8 mm wide, channelled, tapering to a drawn-out tip. Flowering stems up to 30 cm tall; flowers numerous, in a globose head with 1–3 leaf-like bracts at its base; sometimes 2–3 secondary heads arise from its base on short branches.

DISTRIBUTION: North and South Islands as far south as Otago. Local distribution in lowland swamps or brackish ground. Sea level to 500 m.

Juncus gregiflorus

Common rush, wiwi

A tall rush, the stems of which rise from tightly packed clumps and may grow up to 2 m tall. Its bright green, wiry stems are smooth and shining, and can be used to good effect in ornamental horticulture, even though it is such a common plant. Its main use, however, is probably in environmental plantings, particularly re-vegetation.

DESCRIPTION: Forming dense clumps 60–200 cm tall. Leaves none. Stems 2–3 mm in diameter, erect, wiry, smooth and bright, shining green. Inflorescences appearing to be lateral, many- or few-flowered, flowers in small clusters at the tips of branchlets, or condensed into a compact cluster with one or two side clusters, or forming just a single, rounded head more than 1 cm in diameter.

DISTRIBUTION: Kermadec, North, South, Stewart and Chatham Islands. Common in damp pasture and swampy places throughout. Sea level to 1000 m.

Juncus maritimus var. *australiensis*

Sea rush

This is usually a densely tufted species growing to about 1 m or so tall. It has 1–2 leaves, which are similar to the stems but shorter. The inflorescences appear to arise from just below the tip of the stem but, in fact, they arise from the tip. What appears to be the tip of the leaf is really a stiff bract which projects above the inflorescence.

J. maritimus var. *australiensis* does not have any horticultural value and is used for re-vegetation plantings in wetland areas.

DESCRIPTION: Densely or loosely tufted, stems and leaves dark green, 30–100 cm tall. Leaves 1–2, sheathing at the base and similar to the stems. Flowering stems 1.5–3 mm in diameter, rigid; inflorescences appearing to be lateral, open and irregularly branched, branchlets rigid and almost equalling the bract which arises from the base.

DISTRIBUTION: North Island, throughout. South Island, as far south as Okarito and Timaru but also at Dunedin. Chatham Islands. Occurs in brackish water and coastal sandy soils.

Juncus pallidus

Giant rush

A bold, erect species of rush which, because of its size, can be used to make a bold statement in the garden. If there is an opportunity to associate it with the strict and simple lines of modern architecture, it would be an ideal plant. It will thrive in any reasonably moist soil and will also do very well in quite wet places. When well grown it will reach a good 2 m tall.

DESCRIPTION: A very robust plant 1–2 m tall, forming dense clumps. Leaves none. Pale grey-green to deepish green flowering stems 1–2 m tall x 3–8 mm in diameter; pith inside the stems continuous and cobwebby. Inflorescence large, many flowered and loosely spreading or shortened into a more or less dense head; flowers pale. Seed-capsules light brown.

DISTRIBUTION: Throughout the North, South, Stewart and Chatham Islands, in damp or swampy places. Generally never far from the coast. Also in Australia.

Juncus planifolius

Grass-leaved rush

This species has very little to commend it as a garden plant and is probably only useful for environmental or re-vegetation plantings. It will grow in moist soils and will quite freely seed itself about.

DESCRIPTION: A tufted, grass-like species, 30–60 cm tall at flowering. Leaves 15–20 cm or more long, 6–10 mm wide, tapering to a long tip, shallowly channelled or sometimes flattened, light to medium green and of thin texture. Flowering stems up to 60 cm tall; flowers crowded in small, rounded clusters at the ends of a number of branchlets, some of which again branch.

DISTRIBUTION: Found throughout the North, South, Stewart and Chatham Islands, in moist places. Sea level to 900 m. Also occurs in Australia, South America and Hawaii.

LEPIDOSPERMA

Cyperaceae

From Greek *lepis*, a scale, and *sperma*, a seed, referring to the scales around the seed.

Lepidosperma is a genus which is confined to the Southern Hemisphere and contains about 50 species. It consists of perennial herbs, usually with creeping rhizomes, and the flowering stems may be flattened so that they resemble the leaves, or be cylindrical or angled. The inflorescence is paniculate but is often contracted to a simple or branched spike. Three species are native to New Zealand, with the remaining species mainly occurring in Australia.

They can be propagated from seed, but division is probably the easier method.

Lepidosperma australe

An attractive rush-like species with grey- or blue-green stems up to 60 cm or more tall. These are produced from a short, woody rhizome and are usually densely packed. Its brown flower-heads are borne at the tips of the stems and contrast quite well with the colour of the stems. It is easily grown in an open situation in a moist soil. Where a vertical accent or a more formal effect is required, this is a most useful plant. It shows promise of being a good acquisition for the garden.

DESCRIPTION: Rhizome 2–3 mm in diameter, short and woody with dark brown scales. Stems 2–60 cm or more tall, densely clustered, appearing to be cylindrical but actually more or less quadrangular, usually grey- to bluish green. Leaves reduced to brown, sheathing bracts, or the upper 1–2 rather like the stems or triangular in section. Flower-heads spike-like, 1–3 cm x 5–7 mm, brown.

DISTRIBUTION: North Island, throughout. South Island, occurs throughout, but not common in Canterbury and Otago. Also on Stewart and Chatham Islands. Usually in damp places and common in pakihi country. To 900 m.

Lepidosperma laterale

An interesting member of the sedge family with narrow, iris-like green to yellowish green leaves, it usually grows from 60 cm to 1.4 m tall. The leaves have a firm texture, are slightly shiny and their margins are usually reddish or reddish brown. This is quite an attractive species which will grow in an open situation or in light shade. When it flowers the flower panicle is an added attraction.

It needs to be grown with large-leaved plants as a contrast to its narrow and erect foliage. A plant with yellow or variegated leaves would help to emphasise the slender lines of this plant. In the garden it will tolerate poor soils but for best results should have a soil that is reasonably moist.

DESCRIPTION: Growing in coarse tufts from a woody rootstock. Leaves 50–100 cm or more long, 3–5 mm wide, similar to the flowering stems. Flowering stem to 1.4 m tall, 4–6 mm wide, rigid; flower panicle 10–20 cm long, narrow and rigid, spikelets red-brown.

DISTRIBUTION: North Island, from North Cape to about the northern King Country. Usually occurs on poor clay hills or in damp sand. Sea level to 500 m.

LEPTOCARPUS
Restionaceae

The name is derived from the Greek *leptos*, thin or slender, and *karpos*, a seed, meaning 'slender seed.'

A small genus of rush-like plants with the male and female flowers on separate plants. They have creeping rhizomes and their stems are cylindrical, with the leaves reduced to small, persistent sheaths along the stems. The flower spikelets are produced at the tips of the stems, those of female plants being fatter and much more obvious than those of the male.

The genus contains about 15 species, most of which are confined to Australia, but with one species in Southern Chile and one in south-eastern Asia. The single native species is confined to New Zealand.

Leptocarpus similis
Oioi, jointed rush

This is an interesting plant which has a character quite distinct from that of other rush-like plants. Its stems are very slightly zig-zagging, and the small sheath-like leaves which occur at the joints are dark brown at first but become paler with age. Its nature and appearance give it a degree of formality, but it also suits less formal situations equally well. Although it grows naturally in tidal areas, along marshy lake shores and in other coastal damp places, in the garden it will grow quite happily in any reasonably moist, average soil. It forms slowly spreading clumps and, if the clump becomes too large, it is easily kept under control. It is ideal for planting alongside water, in courtyard gardens or surrounded by *Blechnum pennamarina* as a groundcover. It is also quite good as a container plant. Most easily propagated by division.

The early Maori used the stems of oioi as an outer thatching for their whare because they were more durable and superior to other similar plants for that purpose.

DESCRIPTION: A creeping plant, 60 cm to 1.5 m tall, forming dense patches. Stems 1.5–2.5 mm in diameter, usually grey-green, yellowish green or sometimes reddish, with small sheath-like leaves spaced along them at 4–10 cm intervals. Male flower spikelets quite narrow and borne on short stalks; female spikelets have no stalks and are quite fat, red when young but becoming brown with age.

DISTRIBUTION: North, South, Stewart and Chatham Islands. Common in salt marshes, estuarine tidal areas and wet dune hollows. It also grows around the shores of some lakes.

LUZULA
Juncaceae

The generic name is from Classical Latin, possibly from *luciola*, a glow-worm, and *lux*, light, in reference to the shining inflorescences.

These are perennial, grass-like herbs related to the rushes. The leaves are flat, channelled or U-shaped, and often with long white hairs along their margins. Flowers are clustered in single heads at the tips of the stems, or as heads on individual branches.

The New Zealand luzulas are mainly plants of tussock grasslands, subalpine and alpine regions, also very common in rocky situations, with a few occurring around forest margins or in open forest. They are little known in cultivation, and only two species are relatively common in gardens. In the northern hemisphere luzulas are known as wood-rushes, but in this country no common name for them has evolved. In any case, most of our species occur in open country, particularly in mountain regions. While they can be raised from seed, they are all more easily propagated by division.

It is a cosmopolitan genus with about 80 species worldwide, and there are 11 species native to New Zealand.

Luzula banksiana

A variable species with rather broad, grassy leaves which usually have hairy margins and end with a distinctly blunt tip. It is probably of more use as a filler or ground-cover than as a feature plant. It grows best in a moist soil but will also tolerate drier soils and can be grown in a reasonably open situation or in light, partial shade around trees.

L. banksiana comprises a number of varieties, all of which are rather similar, differing only in details of their flowers. One (var. *rhadina*) is more distinct because it has stiff, erect leaves, whereas the other varieties all have drooping leaves.

DESCRIPTION: A rather robust, grass-like plant forming medium-sized tufts 20–28 cm tall. Leaves stiffly erect to drooping, 20–28 cm long, 3–8 mm wide, flat or shallowly U-shaped, margins with scattered, long white hairs. Flowering stems up to 30 cm or more long; flowers in a number of small clusters or occasionally in a single cluster.

DISTRIBUTION: North, South, Stewart, Chatham and Auckland Islands. Two of the varieties may be found in the North and South Islands, three are confined to the South Island, with one of the three occurring as far south as the Auckland Islands. They grow in a variety of habitats from coastal rocks to rock outcrops and bluffs, tussock grasslands or around the edges of swamps and lagoons.

Luzula crenulata

This is an attractive and interesting little species for growing in a pot or a trough garden. Its firm little cushions are always very neat, and its dark green colour contrasts well with yellows or blue-greys. From the way its little leaves stand out stiffly on the stems, it could perhaps be likened to a miniature green hedgehog. It should be grown in a well-drained but moist soil. It is very easily propagated by taking self-rooted pieces of stem from the bottom part of the outside of the cushion.

DESCRIPTION: Forms dark green, dense little cushions, 6–8 cm high and up to 12 cm or more in diameter. Stems much branched and with the remains of the dead leaves long persisting. Leaves (excluding their sheathing bases) up to 8 mm long and 0.5–1 mm wide, deeply U-shaped with the margins inrolled; a few long white hairs on the margins of the sheaths. Flower clusters overtopping the leaves when mature.

DISTRIBUTION: South Island, where it occurs only on the Old Man Range in Central Otago. 1500–1800 m.

Luzula rufa

This consists of rather dense, grassy tufts to about 8 cm high and about 16 cm in diameter. It has narrow, drooping leaves which are usually reddish or reddish green. Being a plant of drier tussock grasslands and open stony places, the leaf colour is best when it is grown in an open situation in a well-drained soil. For short periods it will also tolerate fairly dry conditions. It is a useful plant for a rock garden, or is large enough to be grown in the front of a border, particularly if several are grouped together. The name 'rufa' actually refers to the colour of the scales around the flowers and not to the colour of the leaves.

This species comprises two varieties (var. *rufa* and var. *albicomans*). The leaves of the former are 2.5–6 mm wide, whereas those of the latter are only 1.5–2.5 mm wide and have numerous white hairs along their margins. The variety *rufa* appears to be the only one in cultivation.

DESCRIPTION: Leaves 6–10 cm long, 2.5–6 mm wide, channelled or shallowly U-shaped, with a few long white hairs scattered along the margins; drawn-out tips of the leaves blunt. Flowering heads usually a single rounded head on a 15–30 cm stem.

DISTRIBUTION: South and Stewart Islands in low- to high-alpine areas. Common along the eastern side of the South Island but rare on the western side. Usually in drier tussock grasslands or in open areas in depleted, stony and rocky places. Ascends to 1700 m.

Luzula ulophylla

This is a very distinctive and attractive species which forms tufted little woolly-leaved clumps or patches of silvery white. The leaves are rather deeply U-shaped with the margins slightly in-rolled so that their under surfaces display their conspicuous silvery white hairs. The green to bronze colour of the upper surfaces tends to be hidden by the in-rolled margins. *L. ulophylla* is a plant of dry and exposed conditions, and if treated too well in the garden does not show its true nature. On the other hand, if the conditions are too hard it will not grow as well as it should. It should be grown in a moist but well-drained, gritty soil in full sun. Because of its small size it is more suited for growing in a container such as a pot or trough garden.

DESCRIPTION: A low-growing plant forming cushion-like patches of woolly leaves up to 20 cm in diameter and about 10 cm high. Leaves usually 3–7 cm long and 1–2 mm wide, deeply U-shaped with the margins in-rolled, upper surface green, under surface covered with silvery white, woolly hairs; margins conspicuously hairy. Flower-stems 9–20 cm long; flower-head compact, up to 2 cm long, dark brown.

DISTRIBUTION: Mountains east of the Main Divide in the South Island, from southern Nelson and Marlborough to the Otago Lakes District. Usually occurs in open, stony ground on wind-eroded moraine areas and river flats, or in bare patches in depleted tussock grassland. 300–1800 m.

MACHAERINA
Cyperaceae

From the Greek *machaira*, a dagger, referring to the dagger-shaped foliage.

A genus of perennial herbs with flattened leaves produced in fans after the manner of an iris. The inflorescence is a loosely spreading and often drooping panicle.

There are some 25 species from the West Indies, South America, Hawaii, Malaysia and the Pacific Islands. The single New Zealand species is also found in Malaysia.

Machaerina sinclairii
Pepepe, toetoe tuhara

This species forms large, leafy clumps 50 cm–1 m tall. It is recognised by its flat, bright green, iris-like foliage and, when in flower, by the rusty brown, much-branched, drooping flower panicles. It is a very graceful and distinctive plant which has a great deal of value in the garden. When not in flower, its clumps of foliage are very handsome and have considerable architectural value. Its flowering stems are produced in late spring or early summer and bear a profusion of red-brown or rusty brown spikelets. Much of its colour comes from the filaments of the stamens, which elongate after flowering. They are quite persistent and their effect will last for several months.

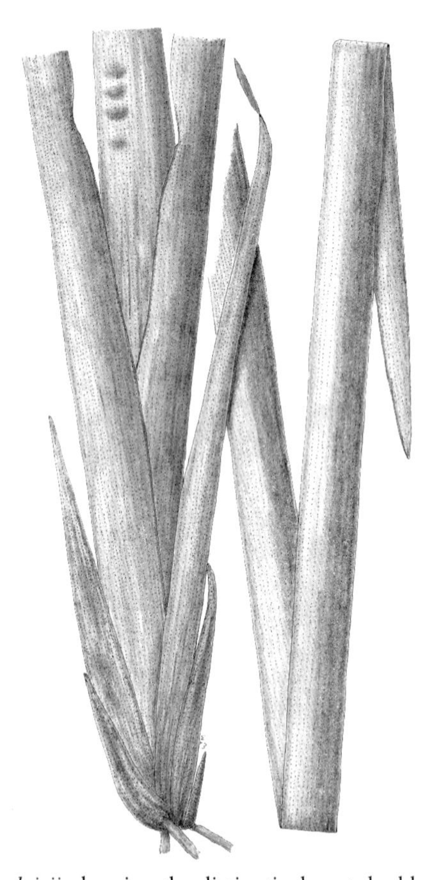

Machaerina sinclairii, showing the distinctively notched bases of the leaves.

It is easily grown in a moist but well-drained soil, in sun or light shade, and will actually tolerate fairly dry conditions when established. It is effective as a single plant or when several are grouped together and can be particularly attractive when planted alongside water. It is quite hardy in lowland districts throughout the country. Propagation is by seed or division.

DESCRIPTION: Leaves 30 cm–1.5 m long, 2–3 cm wide, pale to bright green, shining, quite flat and tough; where the margin meets the sheathing base there is a distinct shallow notch. Flowering stems rather rigid, 50 cm–1 m or more long; panicle 15–40 cm long and much branched. Spikelets numerous in small clusters towards the tips of the branchlets.

DISTRIBUTION: North Island, occurs from North Cape to Hawkes Bay, Taupo and the Whanganui River; then further south to the Ruahine, Kaimanawa and Tararua Ranges. Not uncommon on wet rock faces, stony cliffs, papa clay cliffs and moist road banks. Sea level to 450 m.

MICROLAENA
Gramineae

Derived from the Greek *mikros*, small, and *khlaina*, a cloak, and refers to the very small outer glumes or bracts on the flower spikelets.

A genus of slender perennial grasses with flat or flattish leaves, a creeping or tufted habit and the flowering spikelets arranged in a narrow, lax panicle. The spikelets are laterally compressed and single-flowered.

As currently understood, *Microlaena* is a small genus which is confined to New Zealand and Australia. There are some seven or so native species, all of which are confined to New Zealand.

Microlaena avenacea
Bush rice-grass

A very pleasing grass which grows to 40 cm or so tall. Its foliage is spreading to somewhat drooping and is pale to deepish green, often with a slightly bluish appearance. It is further recognised by its slender and dainty flower-stems, which can be up to 60 cm or so tall and give the plant a very attractive appearance.

Being a forest-dwelling species, it is ideal for growing as a ground-cover under the shade of trees. It prefers a moist soil and the shade should not be too dense. It combines well with ferns and large-leaved herbaceous plants, and is easily propagated from seed, but it can also be divided.

DESCRIPTION: Forms tufts or clumps 40–60 cm or more tall. Leaves 20–40 cm long, 7–12 mm wide, flat, upper surface usually pale and dull, under surface deeper green and shining. Flowering stems rather slender, 30–75 cm tall; flowering panicle 30–60 cm long, sparingly branched with the branchlets nodding.

DISTRIBUTION: North, South, Stewart and Auckland Islands. Fairly common in forests throughout. Sea level to 860 m.

Microlaena colensoi

An easily recognised species which, in cultivation, forms tufts of erect stems and foliage to about 20 cm high. The very long-pointed leaves are up to 15 cm long and are arranged along the stems in two opposite rows so that they lie in the one plane. They are a dull greyish green on their upper surfaces and a darker, somewhat shining green beneath. The flowering stems appear from the tips of the stems.

An interesting species which, unfortunately, always has an untidy look about it because of the way in which the dead leaves remain attached to the lower parts of the stems. It is not too difficult to grow provided it has a moist and well-drained soil and perhaps some shade during the heat of the day. The best means of propagation is by division.

DESCRIPTION: Forms dense tufts or quite extensive patches up to 20 cm or more high. Stems of wild plants trail or lie on the ground before their growing portions bend upwards and become more or less erect; when growing on banks it tends to droop, but the growing portions of stems still distinctively bend upwards; lower portions of stems have the dead leaves remaining attached. Leaves erect and not widely spreading from the stem, 5–15 cm long, 4–5 mm wide, tips long drawn out and very fine. Flower-spike 3–10 cm long, slightly drooping.

DISTRIBUTION: North and South Islands from Mt Egmont, the Ruahine and Tararua Ranges southwards. Often widespread in the wetter ranges of the South Island. 1000–1700 m.

Microlaena polynoda

Bamboo grass, scrambling rice-grass

This is an interesting grass but it can have a rather untidy, scrambling habit. Nonetheless, it is worth growing as an ornamental. It grows in light forest and, while it will tolerate more open conditions in the garden, should still be given some shade. A moist soil in a relatively sheltered position suits it best.

In addition to seed, *M. polynoda* will also propagate itself from self layers where the growing tips of the stems root in to produce new plants.

DESCRIPTION: A much-branched, straggling or scrambling plant with thin, bamboo-like stems which are conspicuously swollen at the nodes. Leaves numerous, rather widely spaced, 7–20 cm long, 3–5 mm wide, flat, margins rough to the touch. Flowering stem 1–3 m long; flower panicle usually reduced to a simple raceme.

DISTRIBUTION: North and South Islands to as far south as Banks Peninsula. Usually in open forest and scrub from coastal to montane areas. Sea level to 500 m.

Microlaena stipoides

Meadow rice-grass, patiti

This rather fine-leaved grass with a creeping and rooting habit usually grows to a height of 30 cm or sometimes up to 60 cm. The stiff and narrow leaves are normally dark green, but at some times of the year they may be more yellowish. It tends to form small patches or clumps and will eventually form a sward. It is one of the few native grasses which can be used for a lawn and will tolerate mowing. If it is mown, care should be taken not to cut too closely and scalp it. Interestingly, when mown it is relatively frost hardy. It succeeds in a wide range of soil types and will stand light shade under trees.

M. stipoides is more suitable for growing in the warmer parts of the country, but it can also be established in cooler districts.

DESCRIPTION: Rhizome branched, creeping and rooting. Stems numerous from the rhizome, erect or ascending, 20–60 cm tall. Leaves 7–20 cm long, 3–5 mm wide, flat, sharply pointed. Flower panicle slender, 7–20 cm long.

DISTRIBUTION: North Island, often abundant throughout. South Island and Stewart Island, more common in the north but in various lowland localities near the sea. Usually in open forest or tall scrub in lowland areas, particularly where the canopy is rather sparse.

Microleana thomsonii

A very small, creeping species which forms loose mats up to 10 cm across with flattened sprays of blue-grey leaves. In cultivation the leaves tend to stand up rather than spread outwards.

It is a plant of alpine bogs and requires a moist peaty soil, preferably with some grit mixed in with it. It is usually tucked away in part of the bog where it is not completely exposed to full sun, and should therefore be given some shade during the sunniest part of the day. Because of its diminutive size it is really only suited for growing in a pot or a trough garden. Personally, I have never found it particularly easy to grow and it is most definitely a connoiseur's plant. It is most readily propagated by division. This is one of our smallest species of grass.

DESCRIPTION: A very distinctive creeping grass with much-branched stems, forming loose mats to 10 cm or so across and with the leaves arranged in flattened sprays. Leaves 0.8–1.5 cm long, 2.5–3.5 mm wide, flattened, upper surface strongly blue-grey, less so beneath. Flowering stem barely extending beyond the leaves; flower-head comprising 2–5 spikelets.

DISTRIBUTION: South Island, where it occurs in south-western Nelson on the Stockton and Denniston Plateaux, Mt Rochfort, and in southern Fiordland. Also on Stewart Island. Confined to alpine bogs and very wet, peaty ground in open areas of tussock-herbfield. 600–1300 m.

OPLISMENUS
Gramineae

From the Greek *hoplismenos*, armed, referring to the rigid awns of the spikelets.

A small genus of trailing annual or perennial grasses with creeping and rooting stems. The leaves are lance-shaped and flat, the inflorescence spike-like, with the spikelets jointed on the pedicel in little clusters. There are about five species, with the solitary New Zealand species being widespread in tropical and subtropical countries.

While it can be propagated from seed, the usual method is from cuttings, which root very easily, or by removing self-rooted pieces from plants.

Oplismenus hirtellus

Basket grass

This is a rather attractive little grass, and although it has ornamental qualities, it is mainly used in re-vegetation plantings. As an ornamental it is useful for growing in hanging baskets and pots, or it can be used as a ground-cover under trees. Generally, it does not form a dense ground-cover and has more of a light and airy nature, although it can be mown to form a dense mat and will tolerate light foot traffic.

Although the native form of this grass is not widely known in horticulture, an introduced variegated clone has been commonly used in greenhouse displays for many years. *Oplismenus* is easily propagated from tip cuttings, and when grown outdoors self-layered pieces can be removed from the parent plant.

DESCRIPTION: Stems prostrate and rooting at the base, ascending above, slender and sparingly branched. Leaves lanceolate, 2–10 cm long, 4–7 mm wide, soft, flat and glabrous or slightly hairy. Flower panicle spike-like, 5–10 cm long.

DISTRIBUTION: Kermadec and North Islands. Occurs throughout in lowland, shaded forest and scrub. In the South Island only in northern Nelson.

OREOBOLUS

Cyperaceae

Derived from the Greek *oreios*, mountain, and *bolus*, a clod, lump or mass, referring to the large cushion-shaped masses.

Small cushion plants of alpine regions, usually growing in bogs or wet and poorly drained soils. They have densely leafy and much-branched stems and form dense or loose cushions, sometimes of considerable extent. Their leaves are rigid, very narrow, and the dead leaves persist on the stems for a long time.

There are three species native to New Zealand and a further nine species, mainly in the Southern Hemisphere but extending to Malaysia, Hawaii, parts of South America and Costa Rica.

Oreobolus pectinatus

Comb sedge

This species received its common name because its rigid leaves lie in the one plane and point out from each side of the stem like the teeth of a comb. It forms cushions about 3–10 cm high and, in the garden, about 12–20 cm in diameter. Its stems and leaves are densely packed so that only the upper portions of the leaves and their tips are visible. The whole plant is a light to medium green colour. It is quite an attractive and interesting plant for growing in a pot or in a trough garden. Being a plant of alpine bogs, it requires a moist but well-drained soil, in a sunny or lightly shaded situation. It is most easily propagated by division.

DESCRIPTION: Forming cushions 1–10 cm high and 50 cm or more across. Leaves arranged in one plane, 12–20 mm long, 0.5–1 mm wide with broad, sheathing bases. Flowers in single spikelets, on short stems, and usually inconspicuous among the leaves; stems elongating at maturity.

DISTRIBUTION: North, South, Stewart, Auckland and Campbell Islands, from Moehau on the Coromandel Peninsula southwards. Usually in bogs, herb-moor and wet depressions in tussock grasslands and herbfields. 600–1700 m.

Oreobolus strictus

This is somewhat similar to *O. pectinatus* but differs mainly in the leaves not obviously being arranged in one plane like the teeth of a comb. It is not so densely branched and tufted, and has longer leaves. Although not quite as attractive as *O. pectinatus*, it is still an interesting plant for growing in a pot or trough garden. Propagation and cultural conditions are as for *O. pectinatus*.

DESCRIPTION: Forming loosely tufted cushions 20–30 cm or more across and up to 10 cm high. Leaves 2.5–30 cm long, 0.5–1 mm wide, sheaths broad and papery. Flowers usually in single spikelets, on stalks that rise just above the leaves.

DISTRIBUTION: North and South and Stewart Islands from the Volcanic Plateau southwards. Often common in bogs or wet areas in grasslands, open forest or scrub. 500-1400 m.

POA
Gramineae

The classical Greek name for pasture or meadow grass.

A large genus mainly from the temperate and colder regions of both hemispheres. The species are quite variable and have flat or rolled leaves but can often be distinguished by the boat-shaped tip to the leaf.

Most of the *Poa* species should be given an annual grooming to comb some of the old foliage out of the tussock. Some species such as *P. astonii* and *P. colensoi* grow much better if the clumps are lifted and divided every three years or so. The divisions soon grow into healthy and better-looking plants.

Poa anceps

This is a tufted species, usually up to 40 cm or so tall, with bright green, flat leaves with the midrib prominent on the under surface. The leaf-sheaths are distinctively purple, and the flowering stems are up to about 70 cm tall. *P. anceps* is a handsome species which is very useful for providing ground-cover under trees where it is difficult to establish other plants. As well as a pleasing appearance, it also has a graceful habit of growth. On young plants the basal growth is more upright with the leaves rather flowing, while older plants are more wide-spreading. When it comes into flower its light and feathery flower panicles stand well above the foliage and are most attractive.

It is quite easily grown in any reasonably good soil and, once established, will withstand moderately dry conditions. It can be propagated from seed but is more easily increased by division. *P. anceps* is a variable species and some very good forms can be selected for cultivation.

DESCRIPTION: A tufted plant of variable habit, often scrambling or trailing, usually about 40–50 cm tall. Leaf-sheaths purple, sharply folded and giving the stems a flattened appearance. Leaves 10–40 cm long, 3–7 mm wide, flat or sometimes folded, light- to slightly blue-green, upper surface dull, under surface shining with the midrib prominent, tip boat-shaped. Flower stem 15–70 cm long; flowering panicle rather open.

DISTRIBUTION: North and South Islands. Common throughout the North Island but, apart from Nelson and Marlborough, rare and local in the South Island. Usually in open forest or scrub but sometimes in grassland. Grows on the forest floor or hanging down rock faces and banks. Mainly coastal but also lowland to subalpine. Sea level to 1070 m.

Poa astonii

Coastal Poa

This is a densely tufted, finely textured, blue-green grass, 20–25 cm tall and, usually, with a spread of 30–40 cm. It is quite a graceful species and rather similar, in general appearance, to *Festuca coxii*. It is a rather lovely blue-green or blue-grey species which is very useful for group planting or for planting along the front of a border. It prefers a soil that does not dry out too much but will tolerate some dry conditions as long as they are not too prolonged. Division is the easiest means of propagation, but it can also be grown from seed.

DESCRIPTION: Forms dense, blue-green tussocks 20–25 cm high. Leaves 15–40 cm long, strongly inrolled, tip sharp and almost pungent. Flower-stems 10–40 cm long, usually inclined; flower panicle stiff and rather open.

DISTRIBUTION: South Island, where it occurs in coastal areas from Banks Peninsula southwards. Also on Stewart, Solander, Snares and Auckland Islands. Grows on rocky coastal cliffs and beaches.

Poa cita

Silver tussock

This is a densely tufted tussock of graceful habit, usually growing to about 50 cm tall, although more robust forms can grow up to 90 cm. Depending on the form, its colour varies from a light tawny yellow to a tawny colour that is toned down by a larger number of green leaves per tussock. The silver tussock is ideal for situations where the size of the garden or lack of space does not permit larger tussock grasses to be grown. It is also useful for associating with the *Chionochloa* species.

It is a rather variable species, and some forms are smaller with finer foliage, while the more robust forms have coarser leaves. These differing forms can be useful for various situations. For best results *P. cita* should be grown in a poorer kind of soil which is not too constantly moist, otherwise it will grow out of character and lose the form which makes it so attractive. In the Auckland area and further north it grows better if planted in exposed and windy situations. It is easily propagated by seed, but selected forms should be propagated by division to make sure that they are true to type.

DESCRIPTION: A dense and rather shiny tussock, of flowing habit, 50–90 cm tall. Leaves 10–60 cm long, 1–2.5 mm wide, heavily inrolled, tip sharp. Flower-stem 30–100 cm long; flower panicle open and rather slender.

DISTRIBUTION: North, South and Stewart Islands, from about upper Thames and Waikato southwards. Common in coastal to subalpine regions in grasslands, scrub and coastal cliffs. Sea level to 1400 m.

Poa colensoi

Blue tussock

This is a small, rather stiff tussock of variable habit and colour. It usually grows to 20–25 cm high and is not very wide-spreading. The leaves are fine and tightly rolled, and vary in colour from a good blue-green to an almost tawny colour. Its flower-stems rise well above the foliage.

Being a plant of mainly drier places it is well adapted for growing in the drier parts of the garden, where it can be used along the front of a border. It is also quite suitable for growing in a rock garden, where it can be used to enhance the habitat for some smaller plants.

This is one species where care should be taken to select and cultivate only those forms which have good foliage colour and a good habit of growth. It is easily propagated from seed, but selected forms should be propagated only by division.

DESCRIPTION: Forming small, rather stiff tussocks, 10–25 cm tall. Leaves 5–30 cm long, 0.7–1mm wide, strongly inrolled and appearing almost cylindrical, green to blue-green in colour, tips sharp. Flowering stems 5–20 cm long; flower panicle 1–5 cm long, open.

DISTRIBUTION: North, South and Stewart Islands from the Coromandel Peninsula southwards. Occurs in lowland to subalpine grasslands, herbfields and rocky places. 300–1500 m, but descends to almost sea level in South Otago.

Poa litorosa

This is one of the larger tussocks, although in cultivation it probably does not grow as large as it does in the wild. It is a densely tufted plant; on young plants the leaves are stiffly erect but as it matures and becomes larger the outer leaves curve outwards and droop. The younger foliage is a bluish green, but because the tips of the leaves are yellowish the whole plant is generally more of a yellowish green in colour.

It is a fairly new introduction into cultivation, from the Auckland Islands, and its ultimate size is not yet known. In nature it grows 60 cm–1.2 m tall and with age rises up on a trunk formed from the old roots and leaf-bases. However, in the garden it probably cannot be expected to achieve such dimensions. It is an interesting and, when well grown, handsome plant which would be well worth having. It associates well with plants with large or bold foliage. Some plants sold under this name are actually *Austrofestuca littoralis*.

It is not difficult to grow in a moist soil, preferably enriched with humus. Its subantarctic habitat ensures that it is quite wind tolerant. Propagation is by seed or division.

DESCRIPTION: A tall, densely tufted tussock, 60 cm–1.2m tall, ultimately rising on a trunk surrounded by a thick investment of dead stems and leaves. Leaves 60–90 cm long, 1–1.5 mm in diameter, strongly inrolled, greyish to yellowish green in colour, tips sharp with long drawn-out points. Flowering stems about as long as or shorter than the foliage; flower panicles 7.5–12.5 cm long.

DISTRIBUTION: Auckland and Campbell Islands.

RHYTIDOSPERMA
Gramineae

From the Greek *rhytidos*, wrinkled, and *sperma*, a seed, meaning wrinkled seed; a mistaken reference. When the name was first given, wrinkled insect larvae in the flowers were erroneously thought to be seeds.

This is an Australasian genus (formerly in *Danthonia*) of mainly small tussocks with fine leaves. One of its distinguishing characters is the prominently hairy leaf ligule; its loose flower panicles, which have several long-awned spikelets, are also a good aid to identification. The flower panicles are suggestive of a miniature version of the flower panicle of some species of *Chionochloa*.

Of the 40 or so species, 18 are native to New Zealand and the remainder occur in Australia. Nine of the Australian species have become naturalised in New Zealand.

Rhytidosperma setifolia
Bristle tussock

This plant forms small, pale green to tawny tussocks, 20–25 cm tall, with stiff, wiry leaves which are quite sharply pointed. In early summer the flowering stems rise above the foliage and bear more or less erect panicles of quite large spikelets, each of which has a conspicuous long awn or bristle projecting from its tip.

When in flower it is a particularly attractive grass which is very useful for growing in dry soils. The flower spikelets are a light golden colour and look very effective with the sun shining on them. Single plants can be quite good, but a group of several plants is much more effective. As well as being tolerant of dry conditions, it is also wind tolerant. It benefits from being lifted and divided every three years or so; the small divisions soon make good plants again.

This species is so easily propagated by division that there is no point in growing it from seed, unless large quantities are required.

DESCRIPTION: Dense, stiff, small tussocks, 20–25 cm high. Leaves stiff and wiry, 25–35 cm long, 0.5–1 mm in diameter, strongly inrolled, pale green to light brown or tawny, sharply pointed. Flowering stems up to 50 cm tall; flower panicles more or less erect, open and few-flowered, spikelets light golden with long bristle-like awns projecting from their tips.

DISTRIBUTION: North and South Islands, where it is widespread in mountain regions throughout. Usually common in drier grasslands, herbfields and rocky places. Lowland to 1700 m.

SCHOENOPLECTUS
Cyperaceae

From the Greek *schoinos*, a rush, and *pleko*, to plait, alluding to its mat-forming rhizomes.

Formerly included in *Scirpus*, this is a genus of annual and perennnial, rush-like herbs with creeping, underground stems. Its aerial stems are rounded or three-angled and are not leafy, the leaves being absent or reduced to basal scales. The flowers are produced at the tops of the stems, but with one or two stem-like bracts arising from just below, the lowest being erect so that the inflorescence appears to be lateral rather than terminal.

The genus is cosmopolitan and contains about 80 species of aquatic or marginal rushes.

Schoenoplectus pungens
Three-square

This is a summer-green plant which is easily recognised by its bluish green, distinctly triangular stems, hence its common name. It normally grows to about 60 cm or so tall and has a creeping root system which quickly forms large colonies. It is sometimes known as American salt sedge because it was first discovered in North America.

It is a plant of estuaries and similar tidal areas, and is used to assist with the treatment of waste water. It grows quite happily away from saline conditions and will succeed in almost any boggy conditions. It is easily propagated by division.

DESCRIPTION: A summer-green perennial with a creeping rhizome which forms rounded, woody tubers. Pale bluish or sea-green stems 30–60 cm or more tall, sharply triangular in section, 2–4 mm in diameter. Inflorescences apparently lateral, of one to four closely compacted spikelets; a bract arising from the base of the spikelets gives the impression that they are situated below the tip of the stem.

DISTRIBUTION: North Island, from the Coromandel Peninsula southwards. South Island, local along coastal areas but absent from Westland and Fiordland. Chatham Islands. Occurs in salt marshes and swamps with brackish water but does occur inland in one or two locations.

Schoenoplectus validus
Kopupu, kuta

This is a tall, creeping, rush-like plant, 1–1.6 m or more high. Its greyish green stems are rounded or slightly three-sided, spongy, and may be as thick as a finger.

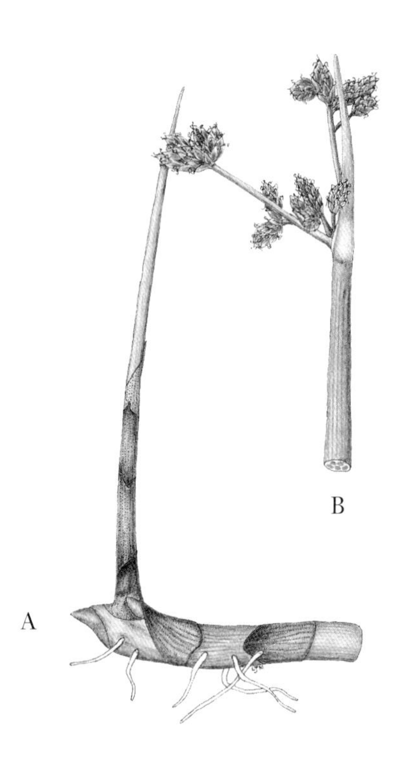

Schoenoplectus validus, showing (A) detail of the creeping rhizome with an emerging young stem; (B) the inflorescence at the tip of the stem.

The flower clusters appear to be below the tip of the stem because a stem-like bract at their bases projects above them.

S. validus is not really a plant for the ornamental garden, although it could be useful for growing in wet soils or around the edge of a large pond. Its main uses are for environmental plantings, where it can be used in re-vegetation projects or for establishing a new wetland area. It is also very useful for planting in areas where waste water requires some form of final treatment. Lastly, and by no means the least important, this species was, and still is, used by the Maori for weaving, and is quite an important plant for them. It is particularly used for weaving mats, and also for hats.

It is easily grown in wet ground or in shallow water and soon commences to spread. In cold districts, at least, it is a summer-green plant which dies down for the winter. It is readily propagated by division.

DESCRIPTION: Creeping rhizome stout, 3–8 mm in diameter, hard and woody. Stems 1–1.6 m or more tall, more or less three-angled or somewhat rounded, greyish green. Leaves reduced to papery basal sheaths. Inflorescence appearing lateral with numerous spikelets in an irregular cluster.

DISTRIBUTION: Throughout the North Island and in the South Island in Nelson, Marlborough, Westland, and in Canterbury as far south as Lake Ellesmere. Usually in brackish, fresh and hot-water swamps, or along the margins of rivers, lakes and ponds. Sea level to 300 m. Also occurs in a number of countries around the Pacific.

SCHOENUS
Cyperaceae

From the Greek *skhoinos*, a rush, in reference to its resemblance to the true rushes, *Juncus*.

This is a genus of rush-like, usually perennial herbs with stems erect, curved or drooping, rounded or sometimes slightly flattened, without joints. The leaves are basal or just above the bases of the stems; sometimes all of the leaves or just the basal leaves are reduced to sheathing bracts. Inflorescences are terminal, forming a head or as solitary spikelets.

The genus comprises about 100 species, of which eight occur in New Zealand. Six of the native species are also found in Australia, with three also occurring elsewhere in the Pacific.

While the species can be grown from seed, division is by far the easiest means of propagation. Forms selected for their good colour should only be propagated by division.

Schoenus apogon

This is a densely tufted plant, 20–40 cm tall. The slender stems are cylindrical, usually bronze-green to reddish. During the winter, in particular, some coppery tones also appear, making it quite colourful. This hardy rush is easily grown and is suitable for planting in moist soils, boggy areas and along the margins of water. For the colour to develop properly it needs to be grown in an open situation.

DESCRIPTION: Stems densely tufted, 20–40 cm long, 1–1.5 mm in diameter. Leaves 4–18 cm long, shorter than the stems or rarely as long as them, very narrow and channelled. Flower panicle of usually two, widely spaced or close clusters of spikelets.

DISTRIBUTION: Throughout the North Island. South Island in Nelson, the Marlborough Sounds and rare in Canterbury. Usually occurs in scrub, on damp grassy banks, around swamp margins and on dry clay hillsides. Sea level to 500 m.

Schoenus pauciflorus

False snow grass

A most attractive species which, especially during the colder months of the year, turns a strong purple-red with the colour showing to advantage when the sun shines through it. In cultivation it usually grows to about 40 cm or so tall and is quite erect, although in the wild the stems are sometimes wide-spreading. It is most effective when associated with yellows and golds or with silvery colours, and when planted as a group, or more widely spaced with a suitable mat plant as a ground-cover between.

It will grow in almost any moist soil in sun and, being a plant of boggy conditions, can also be planted along the margins of water.

DESCRIPTION: A rush-like, tufted plant, erect or the stems rather widely spreading. Stems slender, 30–75 cm long, 1–1.5 mm in diameter, green or deep reddish purple. Leaves reduced to 2–4 basal sheaths, very dark reddish purple. Flower panicles small and compact, 1.5–3 cm long with usually two to six spikelets at the tips of erect branchlets.

DISTRIBUTION: In the North Island from the northern King Country southwards, and throughout the South and Stewart Islands. Also on the Chatham and Auckland Islands. Common in wet places, such as flushes and wet banks in mountain country, but may descend to sea level from Canterbury southwards. 450–1800 m.

Schoenus tendo

This rush-like plant, up to 50 cm high or taller, has crowded stems which are either erect or somewhat drooping. The stems are light green or olive-green and have one or two small spikelets at their tips. It does not have the richly coloured stems of *S. pauciflorus* and is used mainly for re-vegetation plantings. As with the other species, it requires a moist soil.

DESCRIPTION: Rush-like with short rhizomes up to 4 mm in diameter. Stems 50–100 cm tall and about 1 mm in diameter, thickly crowded, erect to drooping, light green. Leaves reduced to sheathing bracts, dark reddish purple. Inflorescence 4–10 cm long at the tip of the stem. Spikelets quite small, dark brown.

DISTRIBUTION: North Island, from North Cape southwards to about Kawhia and the lower Bay of Plenty, and then local further south. Occurs in lowland scrub in wet places.

SPINIFEX
Gramineae

From the Latin *spin*, a spine or thorn, and *fex*, making or producing, in reference to the spiny appearance of the seed-heads.

Spinifex is a small genus of but a few species, which occur in Australia, New Caledonia, Indonesia, Sri Lanka, India, China and Japan; the New Zealand species also occurs in Australia. The species are characterised by their wide-creeping habit, silky-hairy leaves, and the large, globose, spiny seed-heads. The male and female flowers are produced on separate plants.

Spinifex sericeus
Silvery sand grass, spinifex

This is a creeping and rooting grass up to about 60 cm tall, with tufts of leaves arising from the creeping, underground stems. The leaves have strongly inrolled margins and are densely covered with hairs, which give them an attractive silvery, silky appearance. The female plants produce the distinctive large spiny seed-heads, which can be up to 30 cm in diameter.

Silvery sand grass is used primarily to help stabilise sand-dunes. As an ornamental, its value lies with its attractive silvery foliage and the unusual seed-heads of the female plant. It should be planted in a very well-drained (preferably sandy) soil in full sun. Propagation is mainly from seed, but to obtain female plants it should be propagated from portions of the creeping, underground stems. Take a piece which has a tuft of foliage attached or use the actively growing portion from the tip of the stem. It is easily controlled if it starts spreading too widely.

It formerly occurred on coastal sand-dunes from Canterbury northwards, but because of habitat destruction and the introduction of marram grass (*Ammophila arenaria*), it is now much less abundant.

Nowadays, efforts are being made to re-plant this species on dunes in order to restore this valuable sand-binding plant. *Spinifex* (along with pingao, *Desmoschoenus spiralis*) is particularly valuable for stabilising coastal sand-dunes because both species help to build more effectively shaped dunes with a lower profile better adapted for withstanding the destructive effects of wind. Marram grass, on the other hand, builds very steep dunes which can be more prone to wind erosion.

Upon maturity, the large, spiny, ball-like seed-heads eventually break off, to be bowled and bounced along the beach by wind. If they come to rest in a suitable situation, the spines trap sand, which buries the seed-head so that the seeds have a chance to germinate. If the seed-head lodges in a place where it can become saturated by the tide, it will break up, thus giving the seeds another chance to be transported to a situation more suitable for germination.

DESCRIPTION: A perennial grass with creeping and rooting underground stems, often several metres long. Leaves 30–60 cm long, stiff, densely covered with silky hairs and the margins quite strongly inrolled. Male flower-spikes numerous, 5–10 cm long, arranged in a terminal umbel; female heads large, globose, 15–30 cm in diameter, spines numerous and spreading all round.

DISTRIBUTION: North Island, formerly abundant on sand-dunes near the sea. South Island, on Farewell Spit and formerly in Canterbury north of Banks Peninsula.

SPORODANTHUS
Restioniaceae

From the Greek *sporas*, scattered, and *anthos*, a flower, alluding to the dispersion of its flowers.

This genus of but one species, which is confined to New Zealand, has branched, rush-like stems with the leaves reduced to scale-like sheaths. The male and female flowers are on separate plants.

Sporodanthus traversii

This very distinctive, erect, rush-like plant grows 1–2 m or more in cultivation. The stems are 3–10 mm in diameter, cylindrical, shining green, jointed, with pale to medium brown, scale-like leaves at each joint. Along the upper two-thirds of the stem short branches emerge. The flower panicles are at the tips of the stems and are reddish brown.

S. traversii is an interesting and attractive plant which is very suitable for planting in moist to wet soils, or on the edge of a pond. Its shining green stems stand stiffly erect and with their conspicuous jointing are quite distinct. The light reddish brown inflorescences at the tips of the stems are an added attraction. It is quite easily grown in almost any moist or wettish soil as long as it is not heavy clay. In its natural habitat it grows in peaty soils. Because seed is not produced unless both male and female plants are grown, division is the best and most practical means of propagation.

DESCRIPTION: A robust plant, 1–2 m tall, with thick, slowly creeping rhizomes up to 1 cm in diameter. Stems jointed, 3–10 mm in diameter, upper two-thirds more slender and narrowly branched. Leaves reduced to pointed sheaths at each joint. Inflorescences terminal branched, spikelets, pale reddish brown; male and female flowers on separate plants.

DISTRIBUTION: North Island, where it is restricted to peaty areas of the Waikato basin and on the Hauraki Plains. Chatham Islands in wet bogs.

TYPHA
Typhaceae

Perhaps from the Greek *tuphe*, a cat's tail, or *tuphos*, a fen; being the old Greek name for the reed mace or bulrush.

Typha is a cosmopolitan genus of about 10 species of aquatic and marginal herbs with very stout, creeping rhizomes. The leaves usually arise from the base, tufted and in two opposite ranks and are linear, thick and spongy. The flowering stems are not branched; the inflorescence is a terminal spike, cylindrical and appearing thickly brown velvety. The male flowers occur above the female. The solitary New Zealand species is not restricted to this country. In the Northern Hemisphere these plants are often known as reedmace or cat tail, but these names are not used in New Zealand.

Typha orientalis
Raupo or bulrush

A tall and very vigorous, summer-green aquatic plant, growing up to 3 m tall. It has long, strap-shaped leaves up to 3 cm wide and quite spongy, particularly towards the base. However, it is the distinctive, poker-like flower- and seed-heads which immediately identify this plant.

It is a very handsome plant but too vigorous and invasive for any but the largest of ponds. Even then it may need to be kept in check. If it is desired to grow it in a smaller pond for its ornamental value, then it should be planted in a tub or similar container so that it doesn't become invasive. It is probably of more use for environmental plantings such as wetland habitats. It can also be used to assist with the final treatment of effluent water or for stabilising banks alongside water. In a garden situation the dead foliage should be cut off as winter approaches, but in a more natural habitat that is not necessary. It can be propagated from seed, but divisions taken off the creeping rhizomes are much easier.

The flower-heads can be cut and dried for use in floral decorations. They should be cut early in the season while the male flowers at the top of the spike are still in bloom and then air-dried for later use. If cut later in the season the heads may suddenly disintegrate, without warning, once brought into the warmth of a room.

Raupo was of considerable use to the Maori, who cooked and ate the starchy rhizomes and used the pollen from the flowers for baking into cakes. The leaves were important, being much used for thatching roofs and walls, and occasionally they were used for making sails for canoes.

DESCRIPTION: A summer-green plant up to 3 m tall, usually growing in large colonies. Rhizomes 3–4 cm in diameter. Leaves 1–3 cm wide and of a thick and spongy texture. Flowering stems usually shorter than the leaves; inflorescence up to 30 cm or more long, the female part about 2.5 cm in diameter, the male part much narrower.

DISTRIBUTION: Kermadec, North and South Islands, in marshy or swampy places throughout. In the South Island apparently not occurring south of the Clutha River. Also occurs on the Chatham Islands but is believed to have been deliberately introduced.

UNCINIA
Cyperaceae

From the Latin *uncus*, a hook, referring to the hooked process projecting from the ends of the seeds.

This is a genus of herbs that are tufted or with short spreading rhizomes. The leaves are grass-like, shallowly V-shaped or channelled. The flowering stems are slender and more or less three-angled or occasionally rounded. Inflorescences are a simple terminal spike with the male flowers at the top and the female flowers below. The tips of the seeds or nuts terminate in a bristle-like process, the tip of which is sharply bent back to form a hook, which facilitates the dispersal of the seeds.

Only about three of the native species of *Uncinia* have found their way into cultivation, and two in particular are fine garden plants with very effective, reddish coloured foliage. All are easily cultivated in any reasonably moist soil in an open situation. While they can be propagated from seed, division is by far the best means, especially for selected clones. Their hooked seeds have earned them the common name of hook grass or hook sedge. Those who tramp in bush areas will be familiar with the way the seeds hook onto hairy legs or the fibres of clothing.

The genus contains between 40 and 50 species, mostly in the Southern Hemisphere but not in South Africa. Most of the 30 or so native species are confined to New Zealand.

Uncinia egmontiana

This species forms dense tufts or tussocks up to about 40 cm tall and, particularly during the cooler months of the year, the whole plant is a rich reddish or reddish brown colour. Its quite narrow leaves are no more than 2 mm wide, erect at first and gradually arching from about halfway up. With age they tend to bleach towards the tips, which also provides an attractive effect.

It requires a well-drained soil which remains reasonably moist. Better growth is obtained in a situation which is not exposed to too much wind. Its lovely rich colour associates well with blue-grey, grey-green or purplish foliage. A specimen planted amidst a ground-cover of *Acaena buchananii* or *A. inermis* 'Purpurea' would provide a wonderful effect. It also associates well with gold, and a combination of this species with the warm golden orange of *Carex testacea* would also be very effective. When lit by autumn or winter sunlight, it is particularly striking, and consideration should be given to that when positioning it in the garden. It is also useful as a container plant.

DESCRIPTION: A densely tufted plant, 25–40 cm tall. Leaves 20–50 cm long, 1.5–2 mm wide, usually a reddish colour but occasionally green. Flower-stems about 30 cm long, more or less three-angled to almost rounded. Flower-spikes usually 6–9 cm long.

DISTRIBUTION: North Island, confined to Mt Egmont. South Island, from Boulder Lake in north-west Nelson southwards to northern Westland. Also on Stewart Island. Usually in tussock grassland, scrub or bogs. Ascends to 1200 m.

Uncinia rubra

This is somewhat similar to *U. egmontiana* but usually smaller, and the whole plant is a red or reddish brown colour. It is not usually as densely tufted as that species, and its leaves are inclined to be somewhat stiffer.

It is an attractive plant and, being smaller, is more useful if space is too limited to permit *U. egmontiana* to be grown. In the garden it requires similar cultural conditions to *U. egmontiana* and its uses are also similar.

DESCRIPTION: Usually a rather loosely tufted plant 20–30 cm tall. Leaves dark reddish, occasionally reddish green, 15–35 cm long and up to 3 mm wide. Rigid flower-stems up to 35 cm tall, triangular in section; flower-spikes 2.5–6 cm long.

DISTRIBUTION: North Island, from the lower Waikato to northern Manawatu, but mainly on the central Volcanic Plateau. South Island, in Nelson and then east of the Main Divide. Also on Stewart Island. Usually in grasslands, open scrublands and bogs. 450–1400 m but descending to near sea level in Otago and Southland.

Uncinia uncinata

This rather robust and densely tufted species grows to about 40 cm tall, although, depending on conditions, it may grow taller. It has broader leaves than the two former species and they are also more arching. The colour of its foliage can be rather variable and often appears to depend on seasonal and growing conditions, as much as anything. The commonly cultivated form can have foliage of a deep or bright reddish colour, but it can equally be a strong brownish red, and if grown in too much shade, can turn almost green. On the basis of its foliage colour the reddish form of this species is commonly, but incorrectly, sold through nurseries and garden centres as *U. rubra*. The true *U. rubra* is easily distinguished by its very narrow leaves and much smaller size.

Its rich reddish (some describe it as mahogany-red) colour provides an effective contrast to plants with yellow or yellow-green foliage, and it also combines very well with silver foliage. It makes a fine accent plant, either as a single specimen or as a group.

This is a forest-dwelling species and, while the best colour appears to develop in open conditions, it does not like to be planted where it is too exposed to the elements, such as strong and drying winds. It prefers a moist, relatively rich soil but also needs good drainage. One way of getting the best from it is to position it where it receives morning and afternoon sun and is shaded during the middle of the day.

As normally seen in bush areas, *U. uncinata* has green foliage, but occasional plants with reddish green foliage do occur. On Stewart Island forms with good red foliage are quite common, and it may be that one or two superior forms could be selected from there.

DESCRIPTION: A densely tufted plant, 30–50 cm tall. Leaves 20–40 cm or more long, 4–7 mm wide, arching from the base, rough to the touch, double-folded, green to reddish brown. Flower-stems much taller than the foliage and up to 60 cm or more long; flower-spikes 7–20 cm long, flowers densely crowded. Seeds dark brown.

DISTRIBUTION: North, South, Stewart, Chatham and Auckland Islands. Mainly in forests but also in scrub and occasionally in bogs. Often very common in coastal forests. Sea level to 900 m.

Sources of native grasses

Diack's Nurseries Ltd
PO Box 181
Invercargill

Greenwood Nursery
Stringers Creek
RD 1
Richmond 7031

Hains Horticulture
Simpson Road
RD 4
Wanganui

Home Creek Nursery
Hillside-Manapouri Road
Manapouri

Motukarara Nursery
Ridge Road
RD 2
Christchurch

Oratia Native Plant Nursery
625 West Coast Road
Oratia
Auckland

Talisman Nurseries Ltd
Ringawhati Road
Otaki

Taupo Native Plant Nursery
(Terra Firma Ltd)
PO Box 437
Taupo

Index